Praise for *Knowing Me Kno*

Knowing Me, Knowing Them gifts us with a practical, useful, and groundbreaking work for parents and adults in their relationship with children. You will benefit from this book whether you are new or experienced with the Enneagram. Thanks to all three of you for this excellent work.

David Daniels, MD Clinical Professor Emeritus
Stanford Medical School and Enneagram pioneer.

Every parent needs to run and get this book! This book includes 'Parenting strategies for growth' – which is an easy way to apply the learning to connect and stay connected with our children, teens and young adults. Well done!

Diana Sterling, author, *The Parent as Coach Approach*

Finally we have an Enneagram and parenting book that helps us understand how our personality type affects the way we are and aren't effective at the very important task of parenting. I know many parents will find the insights of this book to be invaluable to them, especially if they take seriously the recommended practices at the end of their type chapter.

Margaret Smith, author, *9 Design Principles for Collective Prosperity* and *Intelligence and Money: from fear to love - using the Enneagram to create wealth prosperity & love*

Praise for *Knowing Me Knowing Them*

I attended a presentation on parenting that Tracy gave at an International Enneagram Association Conference in Hong Kong. I really liked her materials and approach and now find Knowing Me, Knowing Them *written with Margaret and Jacqui quite readable and useful. The authors help parents discover and understand the high and low sides of their own parenting styles and offer nine keys to unlocking their child's potential that can be used by all nine styles. I believe parents will find enlightening the insights and suggestions offered and I'm sure their children will be thankful their parents read this book.*

Jerry Wagner, PhD, author, *Nine Lenses on the World: The Enneagram Perspective*

The best Enneagram books come from those who have long experience using the system with real people. Knowing Me, Knowing Them *by Tracy Tresidder, Margaret Loftus and Jacqui Pollock is just such a book. Based on their extensive work with parents and families, the authors provide practical and powerful advice for parents of the nine personality types, as well as nine keys to unlock each child's potential. This book will help those of us who are parents to raise our children with all the love, awareness and skill that this sacred work deserves.*

Peter O'Hanrahan, author, *Embodied Enneagram Handbook*

Knowing Me
Knowing Them

KNOWING ME
KNOWING THEM

Aha!

**UNDERSTAND YOUR
PARENTING PERSONALITY**
by discovering the Enneagram

Tracy Tresidder	Margaret Loftus	Jacqui Pollock

MONTEREY
PRESS

Knowing me, knowing them: understand your parenting personality
by discovering the Enneagram

First published in 2014
by Monterey Press
PO Box 319
Carlton North VIC 3054
Australia
www.montereypress.com

Author contact: info@knowingmeknowingthem.com

Website: www.knowingmeknowingthem.com

Illustrations and cover artwork by Adam Long

Cover design by Fletcher Ross

Typesetting by Sue Balcer, justyourtype.biz

National Library of Australia Cataloguing-in-Publication entry:

Author:	Tresidder, Tracy, author.
Title:	Knowing me, knowing them : understand your parenting personality by discovering the Enneagram / Tracy Tresidder, Margaret Loftus, Jacqui Pollock.
ISBN:	9780987581372 (paperback)
Subjects:	Personality assessment.
	Parenting--Psychological aspects.
	Parents--Psychology.
	Emotional intelligence.
Other Authors/Contributors:	
	Loftus, Margaret, author.
	Pollock, Jacqui, author.

Dewey Number: 155.646

*We dedicate this book to
all the parents, grandparents, teachers and
other adults who do the most important task
in the world of raising children to be the
very best they can be.*

Foreword

by Ginger Lapid-Bodga, PhD

The most important job in the world – being a parent – is one that requires no license, no training, and does not end after 18 years. *Knowing Me, Knowing Them* provides the key to unlocking this high-stress and rewarding job. It will, I hope, be widely read by parents and grandparents everywhere who love their children and want them to be fulfilled and contributing members of a productive and conscious society.

When I read this new contribution to the parenting and Enneagram literature, it was obvious that it was written with care and intelligence, and that the authors know what they are talking about. It's easy to write about parenting if you've never been one, because parenting a child seems easy unless you've been there yourself. However, the three authors of this book – Tracy, Margaret, and Jacqui – have clearly navigated the parenting path, learned its important lessons, and have been able to integrate what they've learned about parenting with their knowledge of the Enneagram so they could share this with the rest of us.

Knowing Me, Knowing Them is a practical book that parents will want to read, share and discuss with their partners and spouses, and keep on their bookshelves for their most challenging parenting moments – and there will be plenty of those. But it is also a great book to give as a present to grandparents, other caregivers, and expectant parents.

It will now be my 'go-to' book for everyone I meet who asks me how to use the Enneagram to become a better parent (and a better person in the process).

Ginger Lapid-Bogda, PhD is an international Enneagram teacher and author of four Enneagram books: Bringing Out the Best in Yourself at Work, What Type of Leader Are You?, Bringing Out the Best in Everyone You Coach *and* The Enneagram Development Guide.

Acknowledgements

Our understanding of this topic has been greatly heightened and enhanced by the experts, teachers, parents and teens we have worked with as parent coaches over the last few years.

This book could not have been written without the assistance of many remarkable people. We are especially grateful for the wisdom and experience of our Enneagram teachers: David Daniels, Peter O'Hanrahan, Ginger Lapid-Bogda, Russ Hudson, Richard Rohr, Jerry Wagner and Roxanne Howe-Murphy. In addition to everything we have learnt from you all, we value the contributions you have made with comments and feedback. A special thanks goes to Ginger who assisted and guided us with content, and also to Margaret Smith who guided us in bringing the 'Nine Keys' to life.

The material in this book has also been informed by Elizabeth Waegle, whose light-hearted yet deep approach in *The Enneagram Made Easy* inspired us to write a book for parents that was fun, informative and helpful.

We would like to thank our editor, David Brewster, who has been incredibly helpful and patient working with three authors! Our magical illustrator, Adam Long, whose creativity and skill at depicting each of the Enneagram types has brought the pages of our book to life. Our typesetter Sue Balcer, who's care and creative eye has produced a fantastic final product. Fletcher Ross, our graphic designer, has done wonders in pulling it all together to create an outstanding cover.

In the background have been many friends and colleagues who have supported us in a myriad of ways. Special thanks to

James Roberts for co-ordinating the book-naming brainstorming evening.

And finally this book could not have been written without the support of our families. Tracy's husband, Mike, and sons, Adam and Ben, have been patient and persevered when other things have fallen by the wayside to ensure the book was finished. Thanks for your encouragement. Margaret's family – husband Peter and children Rachel, Georgie and Jonathan – have consistently shown their enthusiasm and support throughout the exciting and at times challenging process of creating this book. Jacqui's family – parents Ross and Di, husband Jack and children Zoe and Fred – have inspired and encouraged, and shown patience and a sense of humour, whilst Jacqui juggled work and family to follow her passion in creating this book.

Contents

Introduction

"I made him – he's got my DNA, so why oh why is he so different from me?"

Sound familiar?

Or perhaps you hear yourself saying, "She's just like me" or "That sounds just like something my mother would say".

Every parent is fascinated by the personalities of their children, and in particular the ways in which children of the same parents can vary so much. Parents have had this fascination for centuries. For generations we have wondered about the relative influences of 'nature' and 'nurture': how much are our kids 'born that way' and what effect does parenting/birth order/environment/schooling have on their developing personalities?

The truth is that nature *and* nurture both contribute significantly to a child's personality – the research is very clear on this. On the nurture side parental interactions play one of the most important roles, and these interactions depend on each *parent's* personality as much as the child's. Unfortunately, many parents have very little understanding of their own personality. They have little awareness of their habitual behaviours and the way these behaviours affect others, especially their children.

As parents, it is crucial to the flourishing of our children that each of us has a good understanding of our own personality and of the ways in which our behaviours and reactions positively and negatively affect our children. With greater awareness comes greater flexibility and more choice as we respond to the challenges of parenting.

Which is where this book comes in.

When we set out to write this book it was because we recognised that, while there are hundreds … thousands … of parenting books available, the vast majority assume a sort of generic personality on the part of parents. Where there is any differentiation, it is often between the 'commander' parent, the 'soft' parent and the 'rescuer' parent – but the advice is often one size fits all.

Needless to say it isn't that simple.

Being a parent is one of the most challenging, interesting, stressful and rewarding roles we will ever take on. It's one of the toughest jobs we'll do and we set extremely high expectations for ourselves on how we perform in the role. On top of that, today's parent faces a multitude of challenges very different to those of previous generations, including the invasion and distractions of online life, living at a fast pace with little down time, increasing competitiveness, and materialism stoked by ceaseless marketing.

To thrive as effective parents in this world, we need to be able to question our own parenting style in ways that go much deeper than simple questions like "Was I too strict?" or "Am I too easy on him?" We need to be able to get beyond simply comparing ourselves to others. Raising resourceful families in an ever-changing world requires us to have new skills and knowledge and high self-awareness.

We want to give you a fresh perspective on that journey.

We will introduce you to nine different types of parenting personality and help you identify your own type. Each personality type is then separately explored from a parenting perspective, showing its strengths and challenges, its sources of stress and ways in which parents of that personality type can maximise their wellbeing. We'll demonstrate how your particular personality type flavours the way you operate as a parent – for good and not-so-good. We'll share with you a host of things you can do, relevant to your particular personality, to be the best parent you can be. Finally we'll give you some ideas for bringing out the very best in your children, regardless of their own (and still developing) personalities.

A major focus of this book is on self-awareness and 'self-mastery': the ability to understand, accept and transform your own thoughts, feelings and behaviours. We regard these as essential to contemporary parenting. There is no doubt that our parenting skills can be enhanced by gaining a deeper understanding of our own personality, increased ability to control our own reactions and behaviours, and by improving our emotional intelligence.

Our hope is that after reading *Knowing Me, Knowing Them … Aha*, you will find yourself better able to take responsibility for yourself as a parent, and more accepting of who you are. You'll be more aware of your own patterns of thinking, feeling and behaving. Importantly, this will help you spend less time worrying about and judging your parenting approach and more time enjoying the wonderful, all-too-quick experience of raising your children.

Our intention is that your experience of reading *Knowing*

Me, Knowing Them … Aha is unlike that of reading any other parenting book.

Whether you are a parent-to-be, or a parent of babies, toddlers, tweens, teenagers or young adults – it's never too late to start learning about yourself and exploring your personality, enabling you to become the best parent *you* can be.

We wish you many 'aha' moments as you read.

Margaret, Jacqui and Tracy

How to use this book

This book is based on, and structured around, the Enneagram (pronounced "any - a - gram") – a geometric figure that maps nine basic personality types, their patterns of thinking, feeling and behaving, and the relationships between them. Below you can read more about the Enneagram, its history and how it

> **"We don't see things as they are, we see them as we are"**
> – Anais Ni

can be used to improve self-awareness. We will then guide you through three steps designed to help you gain insight into your personality type, the way that type affects your parenting style and how you can use that knowledge to increase your self-awareness, relate more effectively with your children and have them flourish into their best selves.

Step One: **Discover** your Enneagram personality type.

Step Two: **Explore** how your particular Enneagram type affects your parenting style, and ways you can grow with this knowledge.

Step Three: Use our additional resources to help **unlock** your child's potential.

Step One: Discover your personality type

We will start by helping you discover your Enneagram personality type. Knowing this is essential to understanding how your personality influences your parenting style, why you react the way you do in certain situations and why others might respond differently to those situations. It will ultimately help you create deeper connections within your whole family.

Discovering your personality type will help you explore more about your core personality traits and increase your self-awareness. Rather than 'putting you in a box' or 'categorising' you, the Enneagram personality map will help you better understand your own motivations as well as those of other members of your family. It will help you get out of your box.

We will offer you some different methods for discovering your Enneagram type. Regardless of which method(s) you use, be aware that confirming your correct type may take some time. You might quickly find that one type clearly stands out as applying to you. Alternatively, you might find three or four types that could be 'you'. In this case we suggest that you read through the more detailed chapters covering each type in Step Two – there is a good chance you will find that one or two types resonate more with you than the others do. Be patient: finding your type is a journey of self-discovery and sometimes takes a little time.

Step Two: Explore how your type influences your parenting style – and how to grow as a parent

Unlike other parenting books you might have read, in which advice and tips are generically applied without consideration of the different personality types of different parents, this book provides you with comprehensive and precise tips relevant to *your* specific personality type.

Having gained an initial idea about your Enneagram type from Step One, in Step Two you can explore the parenting characteristics of your particular personality type. In this section you will find a chapter devoted to each of the nine types. Reading the chapter for your own type, you will discover:

- how your type positively influences your children
- how your type adversely affects your children
- what is likely to cause you stress as a parent of this type
- what is likely to enhance your wellbeing as a parent of this type
- tips and strategies that will support your growth as a parent of this type.

By reading the chapters about other types, you will be able to compare your own parenting style with those of others. You'll probably start to recognise some of your thought patterns and behaviours showing up in other types as you read through the various chapters. If you have trouble isolating a single type for yourself at Step One, this may help you narrow the choice down. It will also give you some insight into the way you demonstrate elements of other types in different situations (we will explain later what this means).

 **Step Three: Unlock your child's potential**

Every child has the opportunity to flourish into their best self with the support and guidance of a parent who has a high level of self-mastery and an understanding of how to bring out the best in their child. The lessons from steps One and Two will have taken you a good distance down this path.

In Step Three we go further. Every person is part of a complex system and as such the Enneagram recognises each of us has at least a little bit of *every* type within us. Developing all these aspects of yourself is an important part of becoming more complete as a person. In Step Three we apply this concept to the child. We will share with you nine keys to unlocking your *child's* potential, regardless of their own unique (but still developing) personality, so they can flourish into confident, compassionate and courageous human beings.

History and background of the Enneagram

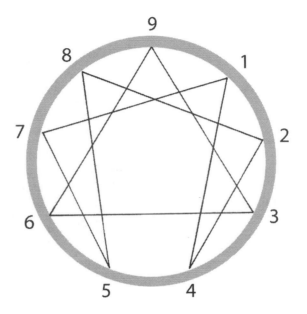

The word 'enneagram' has Greek origins and refers to a shape, or symbol, with nine points. In reference to personality, the Enneagram is a system that studies the motivational differences between people and identifies nine different personality types. Each type is given a number, from one to nine. These nine types and the connections between them are illustrated using an Enneagram symbol (above), with one type placed at each point. Arrows to and from each type represent nine distinct strategies and resource points (we'll explain this later) for relating to oneself, to others and to the world.

While each of us usually has a little of every Enneagram

type within us, one type is usually dominant. The personality associated with each type has its own pattern of thinking, feeling and behaving that arises from an inherent, deep, inner motivation or world view. Our dominant Enneagram type remains the same throughout our lifetime, but the presenting characteristics may either soften or become more pronounced as we grow and develop.

The history of the Enneagram system of personality types is somewhat mysterious and controversial. Elements of the Enneagram and related teachings about psycho-spiritual growth can be found in many of the world's major mystical spiritual traditions, including esoteric Christianity, Hinduism, Judaism, Buddhism and Sufism.

The contemporary version of the Enneagram symbol was first brought to the attention of the modern world by Russian G. I. Gurdjieff, the originator of a school of spiritual work in the early 1900s. Bolivian Oscar Ichazo is attributed with assigning different personality types to each of the nine positions on the diagram, creating the Enneagram of Personality as we know it today.

Claudio Naranjo, a Chilean-born, American-trained psychiatrist who had explored theories of personality extensively, studied with Ichazo and further developed the latter's teachings, articulating the nine types in Western psychological terms. Naranjo then brought his understanding of the Enneagram system to University of California Berkeley in the early 1970s, where he taught it to students in the context of his own program of self-development work.

The current use of the Enneagram incorporates further development by various others, including Helen Palmer, David

Daniels, Don Riso, Russ Hudson and Jerry Wagner. They published the first widely read books on the subject in the late 1980s and early 1990s.

The best way to understand the Enneagram in practice is to identify your own type and its dominant characteristics. From there you will start to recognise the distinctions between your type and the others and begin to get a feel for how your mind works, what your heart feels and what your body experiences. But first let's briefly introduce the nine types.

The nine types

Below are broad descriptions of the nine Enneagram personality types.[1]

In these descriptions we make reference to levels of mastery, or 'self-mastery'. By this we mean how developed our self-awareness is. At lower levels of self-mastery we tend to react to negative situations with unproductive behaviour. At higher levels of self-mastery we respond to these same situations in productive and flexible ways. We might find we respond at different times with low, medium or high mastery. We will discuss this and related terms in more detail later. We also use the term 'wake-up call', which is a clue or warning that we could be moving to a lower level of self-mastery (see Riso & Hudson 1999, p.80). Becoming aware of the primary wake-up call associated with your type is one of the most powerful ways of using the Enneagram in your daily life.

---

1 With thanks to the work of Helen Palmer, David Daniels, Russ Hudson and Don Riso

Type One: The perfectionist and the organiser

The principled, idealistic type. Ones are ethical and conscientious, with a strong sense of right and wrong. They are teachers and crusaders, always striving to improve things but afraid of making a mistake. Well organised, orderly, and sometimes fastidious, Ones try to maintain high standards but can slip into being critical and perfectionist.

High mastery: Ones are wise, discerning, realistic and noble, as well as morally heroic.

Low mastery: They typically have problems with repressed anger and impatience.

Wake-up call: Feeling a sense of personal obligation to fix everything themselves.

Type Two: The helper and the giver

The caring, supportive type, Twos are empathetic, sincere and warm hearted. They are friendly, generous and self-sacrificing, but they can also be sentimental, flattering and people pleasing. They are driven to be close to others, and they often do things for others in order to be needed.

High mastery: Twos are unselfish and altruistic and have unconditional love for themselves and others.

Low mastery: They typically have problems taking care of themselves and acknowledging their own needs.

Wake-up call: Believing that they must go out to others to win them over.

Type Three: The achiever and the motivator

The adaptable, success-oriented type. Threes are self-assured, attractive and charming. Ambitious, competent and energetic, they can also be status conscious and highly driven for personal advancement. Threes are often concerned about their image and what others think of them.

High mastery: Threes are self-accepting, authentic and everything they seem to be – role models who inspire others.

Low mastery: They typically have problems with workaholism and competitiveness.

Wake-up call: Beginning to drive themselves for status and attention.

Type Four: The creative and the individualist

The expressive, introspective type. Fours are self-aware, sensitive, reserved and quiet. They are self-revealing, emotionally honest and personal, but they can also be moody and self-conscious. Withholding themselves from others due to feeling vulnerable and defective, they can also feel disdainful and exempt from ordinary ways of living.

High mastery: Fours are inspired and highly creative, able to renew themselves and transform their experiences.

Low mastery: They typically have problems with self-indulgence and self-pity.

Wake-up call: Holding on to and intensifying feelings through the imagination.

Type Five: The observer and the investigator

The objective, cerebral type. Fives are intense, alert, insightful and curious. They are able to concentrate and focus on developing complex ideas and skills. Independent and innovative, they can become preoccupied with their thoughts and imaginary constructs. They then become detached, yet highly strung and intense.

High mastery: Fives are visionary pioneers, often ahead of their time and able to see the world in an entirely new way.

Low mastery: They typically have problems with isolation, eccentricity and nihilism.

Wake-up call: Withdrawing from reality in concepts and mental worlds.

Type Six: The questioner and the loyalist

The committed, safety-conscious type. Sixes are reliable, hard-working and responsible, but they can also be defensive, evasive and highly anxious – running on stress while complaining about it. They are often cautious and indecisive but can also be reactive, defiant and rebellious.

High mastery: Sixes are internally stable, self-confident and self-reliant, courageously supporting the weak and powerless.

Low mastery: They typically have problems with self-doubt and suspicion.

Wake-up call: Becoming dependent on something outside the self for guidance.

Type Seven: The enthusiast and the epicure

The busy, productive type. Sevens are versatile, optimistic and spontaneous. Playful, high-spirited and practical, they can also be overextended, scattered and undisciplined. They constantly seek new and exciting experiences, but they can become distracted and exhausted by staying on the go.

High mastery: Sevens focus their talents on worthwhile goals, becoming joyous, highly accomplished and full of gratitude.

Low mastery: They typically have problems with superficiality and impulsiveness.

Wake-up call: Feeling that something better is available somewhere else.

Type Eight: The asserter and the protector

The powerful, dominating type. Eights are self-confident, strong and assertive. Protective, resourceful and decisive, they can also be proud and domineering. Eights feel that they must control their environment, often becoming confrontational and intimidating.

High mastery: Eights are self-mastering – they use their strength to improve others' lives, becoming heroic, magnanimous and sometimes achieve great things

Low mastery: They typically have problems with allowing themselves to be close to others.

Wake-up call: Feeling that they must push and struggle to make things happen.

Type Nine: The accommodator and the peacemaker

The easygoing, unassuming type. Nines are diplomatic, accepting, trusting and stable. They are good natured, kind hearted and supportive but can also be too willing to go along with others to keep the peace. They want everything to be without conflict, but can tend to be complacent and minimise anything upsetting.

High mastery: Nines are indomitable and all-embracing; they are able to bring people together and heal conflicts.

Low mastery: They typically have problems with being passive and stubborn.

Wake-up call: Outwardly accommodating themselves to others.

Step One:

Discover your
personality type

Discover

How to find your Enneagram type

Unlike many other personality-type models, determining your Enneagram type does not rely on completing a single questionnaire. There are in fact a number of ways to approach the task. We would like to offer you three options. If one test is inconclusive for you, another may help you 'narrow the field'.

Option 1   Read the nine descriptive paragraphs below – instructions are provided on page 21.

Option 2   Complete an online questionnaire at this book's website: visit www.knowingmeknowingthem.com and follow the prompt 'Take a free test'.

Option 3   Download and use the smartphone app called 'Know Your Type', developed by Ginger Lapid-Bogda. The app is available for iOS (Apple) and Android devices. Details and links can be found at www.enneagramapp.com or on the app store for your phone.

Note that none of the options for determining your Enneagram type, nor any of the other discussion in this section, specifically relates to parenting styles. For now we are concerned only with you gaining greater self-awareness. We can then put this awareness to good use in Step Two.

The 'Nine Descriptive Paragraphs' test[2]

Below are nine paragraphs that describe nine different perspectives of the world. None of these viewpoints is more valid than any other. Each paragraph is a simple snapshot of one of the nine Enneagram personality types, describing the way someone of that type tends to see the world, their style

---

2 With thanks to David Daniels for allowing us to use his reliable and scientifically validated paragraph test.

of attention, dominant mental and emotional biases, central preoccupations and positive attributes. No paragraph is intended to be a comprehensive description of an individual's personality – use them as a starting point for identifying your Enneagram type.

Instructions

1. Read all nine descriptors below.
2. Reflecting on what you have read, try to pick the three paragraphs that seem to most closely describe your personality. It is not unusual to find elements of each paragraph you can relate to, but your goal here is to choose the three that seem most like you.
3. In the table below, rank these paragraphs from 1 to 3, with 1 being the paragraph that seems most like you, 2 the one next most like you, and 3 the third most like you. In making your selections, consider each paragraph as a whole rather than considering any sentence out of the context of its paragraph. Ask yourself, "Does this paragraph as a whole fit me better than any of the other paragraphs?"

If you find it difficult to choose the three paragraphs that best define you, think about which ones someone close to you might select if they were asked to describe you. If you have already been doing some personal development work, you may find it helpful to think about yourself in your mid-twenties – personality patterns are usually most prominent before we begin work on personal development.

As you read through the descriptors below and consider

how well each type applies to you, remember that each type has its gifts and challenges and *no type is 'better' than any other.*

Use this table to record your top three paragraphs. At the end of the chapter we will reveal which paragraph is associated with which Enneagram type and you will be able to complete the third column.

	Paragraph letter	Enneagram type
Most like me		
Second choice		
Third choice		

Paragraph A:

I am a sensitive person with intense feelings. I find richness and meaning in authentic relationships. I feel happiest when I am deeply connected, and the search for emotional connection has been with me all my life. I'm drawn to the arts in various forms – my artistic appreciation is for the sophisticated and unique. I feel different from everyone else. I often feel misunderstood and lonely. I'm willing to experience the sadder parts of life – in fact to me melancholy has a wistful quality. I have been criticised for being overly sensitive and for over-amplifying my feelings. I can react strongly with anger or withdraw with sadness – people don't understand me and might think I'm being over dramatic. I have difficulty fully appreciating present relationships because of my tendency to want what I can't have and to disdain what I do have. I sometimes wonder why other people seem to have better relationships and happier lives than I have. I'm creative and expressive and I find the ordinary boring.

Paragraph B:

I am very good at helping people resolve differences because I can usually see and appreciate all points of view. This ability to see the advantages and disadvantages of all sides can make me appear non-judgemental, but also indecisive at times. This tendency sometimes leads me to be more aware of other people's positions, agendas and personal priorities than of my own. I do not like conflict and it takes a long time for me to show my anger directly. It can sometimes be quite explosive when I do! I engage in a number of activities while sometimes getting so involved in one activity that I forget about other things I am supposed to do. My attention can also be diverted to unimportant, trivial tasks as I avoid the one that is most important. I am easygoing, pleasing and likeable. I seek a life that is comfortable and harmonious and for others to be accepting of me.

Paragraph C:

I am responsible, hardworking and constantly trying to improve myself and the world around me. I am a principled, ethical and moral person with high standards that I like others to meet as well. I often feel personally responsible for making things right and am quick to judge others if they don't meet my expectations. I spend a lot of energy trying not to make mistakes. I seek perfection and am disappointed in myself when I don't achieve it. I may come across as being overly critical or demanding of perfection, but it's hard for me to ignore things that are not done the right way. I tend to control and repress my anger, and I will rationalise and justify my thinking about how I am right and others are wrong. This can create tension and rigidity in my body, tone of voice and behaviour.

Paragraph D:

I think that to succeed in life you have to be strong and know how to defend yourself. I am assertive and have the energy and confidence to overcome most obstacles. I am decisive and have a good instinct; I am quick to respond. I believe that it is a hard and unjust world and I need to protect innocent people, especially when an injustice is being done, yet I have trouble tolerating weakness in others. I am magnanimous, having a big and gentle heart. I am a no-nonsense kind of person and if I do not agree with those in authority I will step in and take control. It is hard not to display my feelings when I am angry and sometimes an emotional outburst scares people off. I can appear over confident – almost too big to fail – and this can be my Achilles heel. I also have a gentle, caring side that I don't show very often in case I am taken advantage of.

Paragraph E:

I'm a very busy person and I get lots done. I usually have more to do than I can fit into my time. I'm motivated by a need for success and achievement. It's important that I try to be the best at what I do. Because I'm results orientated I usually achieve any goal I set for myself. People recognise me for what I can achieve. I identify strongly with what I do, because I believe that who and what you are is important – that people value what you achieve. When I get super busy, I might set aside feelings and self-reflection in order to get things done. I find it hard to just sit and do nothing. I get impatient with people who don't use my time or their time well. When someone is completing a project or a task too slowly, I wish I could step in and take over. I like to feel and appear 'on top' of any situation and for people to view me as confident and successful. I'm a good competitor and I am also a good team player.

Paragraph F:

One of my greatest strengths is my sharp and incisive mind. When I imagine something is threatening my safety or security, I go into high-gear mentally. I can usually spot what could be dangerous or harmful and may experience as much fear as if it were really happening. I may either avoid danger or approach it head-on; sometimes I go into action with little hesitation and don't experience much fear. I have an inquisitive mind, which allows me to access keen insights or intuition. I would like to be more certain but I generally doubt or question the people and things around me and see the shortcomings in the views others put forward. I have a good sense of humour that is somewhat off-beat. Trusting others is a central issue for me and I often scan my environment to determine whether a danger may be forthcoming. I am suspicious of authority and not particularly comfortable being seen as the authority. Once I commit myself to a person or an organisation I am very loyal to it. I am usually active in supporting underdog causes because I see what is wrong with the generally held view of things.

Paragraph G:

I enjoy my own company and am not concerned about spending time alone. It actually gives me a time to recharge and gather more knowledge. I have a clear, objective mind and am a very perceptive observer. Learning new information and understanding how life works fascinates me. I dislike social gatherings and find talking about irrelevant things annoying. I see life objectively, without much emotional reaction. I try to minimise hassles in life, as well as any physical and emotional needs. I conserve energy by withdrawing, or sometimes by provoking with sarcastic comments, when I feel intruded upon. I understand how things work and like to be competent and master things I am interested in. I have a very active mental life and am never bored when I am alone.

Paragraph H:

My greatest strength is that I instinctively know what someone else needs, even if I don't know them. I am warm hearted, friendly and generous and make people feel special and loved. I value good relationships and work hard at developing them. It can be difficult for me to resist helping others, or to say no if asked. I can then become overwhelmed with all I have taken on – I can put so much energy into caring for others that I don't take care of myself. I find it difficult to ask for help directly and tend to manipulate others to get what I want. I like to be seen as warm hearted and a good person, but when I feel taken for granted or my efforts go unappreciated I can become emotional or demanding.

Paragraph I:

I am an optimistic and spontaneous person who enjoys coming up with new and interesting things to do. I have a very active mind that quickly moves back and forth between different ideas – often too quickly for others to follow. I like to get a global picture of how all these ideas fit together, and I get excited when I can connect concepts that initially don't appear to be related. I like to work on things that interest me, and I have a lot of energy to devote to them. I crave the stimulation of new ideas. I love to be in on the beginning of a project, during the planning phase, when there may be many interesting options to consider. I have a hard time sticking with unrewarding or repetitive tasks. When I have exhausted my interest in something, it is difficult for me to stay with it. I want to move on to the next thing. If something gets me down, I prefer to shift my attention to more pleasant ideas. I like to keep my options open; I don't like the feeling of being restricted or boxed in. I'm upbeat and happy and believe people are entitled to an enjoyable life.

The following are the Enneagram types associated with each of the paragraphs/descriptors above. Use this table to complete the third column of the table above. And don't forget that if you are having difficulty identifying your most likely types, you can try one of both of the other typing methods described earlier.

27

Paragraph	Enneagram type
A	4
B	9
C	1
D	8
E	3
F	6
G	5
H	2
I	7

Discover

Layers of the Enneagram

The Enneagram offers layers of self-knowledge that go much deeper than the allocation of a single type. While it is beyond the scope of this book to delve into those layers in any detail, a basic understanding will give you more self-awareness and this will assist you in developing mutually respectful relationships between yourself and each of your children.

Note that at this point, having identified your own Enneagram type, you may prefer to jump past the rest of this step and start on Step Two. You can return to this section later when you are ready to explore the Enneagram in some more detail.

The nine types and the centres

The types are often presented in groups of three (triads), based on which of three major personality components – or 'centres' – most influences each type: *feeling, thinking* or *instinctual*. Below are descriptions of the common characteristics of the types associated with each centre, and the ways in which that centre influences its types.

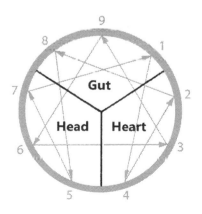

29

The Feeling, or 'Heart', Centre: Types 2, 3, 4

The Enneagram 'feeling' or 'heart' centre is about maintaining a personal identity. Those of this centre want others to respond to them in very specific ways and create an image to get the desired response. By staying attuned to the moods and feelings of others, they can maintain a feeling of connection with them. All three types can end up feeling not valued for who they really are and, although outwardly confident, they can experience feelings of emptiness and sadness.

Twos – the helpers and givers. Twos are caring, interpersonal types who are generous and sensitive to the feelings of others. They maintain an image of being loving and selfless.

Threes – the achievers and motivators. Threes are adaptable and success orientated and are practical and competent. They like to be seen in a good light.

Fours – the creatives and individualists. Fours have a rich and dramatic interior life. They are creative with a capacity to empathise with others. They also have a strong need to express themselves.

The Thinking, or 'Head', Centre: Types 5, 6, 7

The Enneagram 'thinking' or 'head' centre is about finding an inner sense of guidance and support. Those of this centre are always thinking, and they value facts, information and ideas. They seek security to help them deal with their feelings of fear and anxiety.

Fives – the observers and investigators. Fives like to acquire knowledge and achieve genuine insights and understanding. This helps them to feel competent. They protect themselves from intrusion and demands by seeking privacy and becoming self sufficient.

Sixes – the questioners and loyalists. Sixes are reliable, hardworking and responsible and have the ability to bring loyalty to persons, groups and causes. They notice any potential danger and prepare for every possible scenario to feel safe.

Sevens – the enthusiasts and epicures. Sevens are active, enthusiastic and productive. They have the ability to bring joy and optimism into all life's circumstances and plan for positive possibilities to avoid feelings of discomfort like pain, anxiety and boredom.

The Instinctual, or 'Gut', Centre: Types 8, 9, 1

The Enneagram 'instinctual' or 'gut' centre is about maintaining a sense of one's self and autonomy. Those of this centre filter the world through physical sensations and gut instinct. They are concerned with power and justice and want to control their world without being controlled by it. They have an underlying feeling of anger or rage, which is not always outwardly expressed.

Eights – the asserters and protectors. Eights present as strong and powerful and have the ability to confront whatever needs to be confronted and say what needs to be said. They express their anger easily.

Nines – the accommodators and peacemakers. Nines are accommodating and easygoing. They have the ability to bring a sense of peace and harmony to stressful and discordant situations. They repress their anger to avoid feelings of conflict.

31

Ones – the perfectionists and organisers. Ones are principled and idealistic and have the ability to see clearly what makes things good, just, right and proper. They resist showing anger because they see it as a character flaw.

All of us, regardless of our type, have access to all three centres. However, a bit like a three-legged stool, our tendency is to be unbalanced, with strength in one centre over the others – the centre associated with our type. Our challenge is to maximise our growth potential, which is best served by developing each of the three centres and becoming more balanced. This is something that will be explained in greater detail further into this book.

Variations of type: Wings and arrows

The 'flavour' of your type, as it applies uniquely to you, has many influences. These include your cultural values, your family of origin, and the relationships you had with nurturing and protective figures during your developmental years. Your personality is particularly influenced by the types on either side of your own (called the 'wings') and the types connected to your own (called the 'arrows'), which we will explain here.

The wings

One of the unique characteristics of the Enneagram, when compared with other personality typologies, is that the Enneagram recognises a high degree of individuality. No one is purely of their type. All of us, to a greater or lesser degree, display aspects of Enneagram types other than our own

32

dominant type. (You probably will have noticed this in recognising facets of yourself in some of the paragraphs above that did not, as a whole, describe you very well.) In particular, our unique personality is influenced to some degree by the types found either side of our own in the Enneagram symbol. These are known as 'wings'.

Each Enneagram type has two possible wings. Take a look at the arrangement of the symbol and you'll see you have a type on either side of yours – these are your type's potential wings. For example, if you are a Type Seven, you might have a Six wing or an Eight wing.

One wing may be dominant. If you have a dominant wing it flavours your personality. Understanding this can become a great resource beyond knowing the strengths and potential of your type. Once you know your primary type, go back and read through the descriptors of your wings: the types shown on either side in the diagram above. For example, if you are a Type Nine, read the descriptors in Step One of Type Eight and Type One. While you may notice that you have some characteristics of each of your wings, one of them may feel more dominant than the other.

In Step Two, we have noted the influence on each type of its wings. These will give you an extra level of understanding of the way your type affects your parenting style.

The arrows

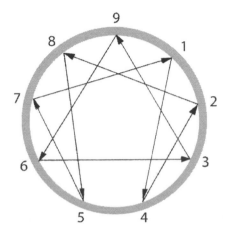

Another characteristic of the Enneagram is that rather than 'putting you in a box', it shows you how to get out of the box you are in. In other words, it provides important guidelines for personal growth and development – what we call increasing 'self-mastery'. Increasing your self-mastery means developing your skills of self-management, emotional maturity and personal responsibility.

The guidelines for growth and development are illustrated by the lines and 'arrows' pointing towards and away from your type on the Enneagram symbol. On the symbol (above) you will notice lines connecting your type to two other types; one of these lines has an arrow pointing away from your type and the other points towards your type. For instance, Type Seven is connected by lines to Type One (pointing away) and Type Five (pointing toward).

34

The lines and arrows give an indication of how – under certain circumstances – our behaviour can change from what is typical for our primary type, instead taking on aspects of our connected types. Let us explain.

In situations of stress or when under pressure (with which most parents will be familiar), many people will exhibit negative aspects of the type shown in the direction of the arrow. In other words, Sevens start to behave with some of the negative characteristics of Ones. You can test this yourself: find the type at the end of the arrow pointing *away* from your type – we call this the 'stress point' – and read the descriptor for that type. See if you can identify aspects of that type that sound like you when you're stressed. The frequency and extent to which this shift happens is an indicator of a person's level of self-mastery. Low levels of self-mastery lead to reduced energy and behaviours that disconnect you from a sense of wellbeing (i.e. by moving you away from your type towards your stress point). This can have detrimental effects on your relationships.

> *For example, when a Type Seven is under stress they will often take on the negative characteristics of a Type One. They move from being optimistic and creative towards being critical and perfectionistic.*

Improving your self-mastery – in part by better understanding your personality – will give you greater awareness of when you might be moving towards your stress point – before you get there. You will start to recognise when you use the negative characteristics of your type's stress point. With this awareness you will increasingly be able to handle challenges and pressure without shifting to that stress point.

The contrasting situations are when we are feeling particularly secure or relaxed. At these times we tend to take on positive qualities of the type at the end of the other connecting arrow – the arrow pointing towards our own type. We say that the positive aspects of that type start to fuel our dominant type. That is, secure Type Sevens behave with some of the positive aspects of Type Fives, and so on. We call this our type's 'security point'. For example, a Type Seven may slow down, become less distracted and more focused and centred. They become more content to spend time on their own. Again you can test this by rereading the descriptor associated with your own security point. When we move towards our security point we often feel relaxed and happy as we tap into the positive energy of that type. As we increase our self-mastery, we are able to make this transition more easily, and this helps our personality become more 'integrated' and complete.

While we do have a tendency to go in the direction of the arrow when we are under stress, and against the arrow when we feel secure, we actually have access to both the positive and negative aspects of the Enneagram types at the ends of our arrows. With ongoing development, we can use all of these as resources to increase our level of self-mastery.

As you read through the chapter for your type in Step Two, it is worth bearing in mind the variations of your type represented by its wings, and the shifts represented by its arrows. These will remind you that very little is 'black and white' when it comes to personality – even less so when it comes to parenting.

36

Self-awareness and emotional intelligence

Hopefully by this point you have a reasonable idea of what your Enneagram type might be. We hope you also understand that your type cannot be precisely described, in the sense that each of us represents a unique version of our type, and that we can present different types to the world, depending on how secure or stressed we are.

With this knowledge established, you are well placed to start a journey of self-awareness and emotional intelligence. And as a parent you will have ample opportunities to build your skills in both of these!

Self-awareness is the willingness and capability to step back from your initial reaction to situations and to observe what is happening inside yourself emotionally – *before* you respond. Most of us react habitually to many of the situations we experience. For example, imagine one of your children leaves a toy in the hall that you trip over. This may trigger an immediate angry reaction from you. You raise your voice, to which your child responds by raising theirs and, before you know it, your 'conversation' has escalated into a screaming match that leaves both of you frustrated and unhappy.

While your anger is a common reaction to this situation, it is not the only option. You can learn to recognise behaviours – like yelling – that are habitual and that happen with little conscious decision on your part. You can also learn that many of these reactions are not resourceful responses: they do not bring about a desired or positive result. We call these unconscious, unresourceful, 'below the line' reactions. The diagram below lists a number of them.

Discover

Discover

Above the line	**support** **acknowledge** **appreciate** **respect** **inspire**	**be decisive** **enthuse** **focus/attend** **accept**	**Take personal responsibility**

Line of choice

Below the line	defend deny justify blame intimidate	pessimistic manipulate be cynical criticise	**Place responsibility on others**

However, if you practise taking a breath when you feel anger rising up, or another below-the-line response surfacing, you can learn to notice that reaction before it shows itself. This gives you a moment to consider and choose a better, more resourceful response. While it is natural to feel angry about the toy being left on the floor, choosing an above-the-line behaviour to respond with will be more productive. Every time you choose a more resourceful behaviour you take another step forward in your self-mastery.

Emotional intelligence (sometimes called EI or EQ) is having the ability to recognise, understand and manage emotions in ourselves and others. Improving in these areas can build self-confidence and give you a more positive and stronger sense of your own worth. EI helps us relate to others with more empathy and, therefore, more effectively. Parents with high emotional intelligence are more present to their children and develop stronger relationships with them and have a more positive influence.

A high level of self-awareness, along with a good under-standing of your personality and what motivates your behaviours, is essential to developing your emotional intelligence. The Enneagram is a wonderful tool to help you achieve these things. By becoming aware of what motivates your personality type to react and behave in certain ways – combined with the awareness to be able to step back and observe what is happening in you – you can learn to choose those 'above-the-line' behaviours that are the most resourceful for you – and to avoid those 'below-the-line' behaviours that tend to derail you. This is especially important during times of stress, when you are most likely to display your least helpful behaviours.

Typing and children

Human nature determines that we have a tendency to want to categorise objects and data – including ourselves. As a parent, it follows that as you get curious about yourself by determining your Enneagram type, you will start thinking about the Ennea-gram types of your children too.

We would caution against either trying to distinguish your children's types yourself or having them try to discover their own Enneagram type. We offer this advice for a number of reasons.

- A child's personality is still very much in develop-ment. Their adult personality will be determined by a combination of nature (which they were born with) and nurture (how they interact with the environment that accompanies them through childhood). Our job as parents is not to place a child in a box, but rather to support and guide them, helping their nascent personality to flourish and 'fill out' as they grow.

- Attempting to categorise at too early an age can lead to stereotyping – in effect it can become a self-fulfilling prophecy. This could be particularly troublesome were we to mistype our child at an early age.
- Applying a type to a child can be misused as an excuse for our own behaviour, or as a source of blame for their behaviour.
- Even with older children (in, say, their late teens), it is crucial that the child's level of cognitive development is considered in their capacity to understand Enneagram types and their use for psychological and spiritual development.

On top of these considerations, it is worth remembering that your first task here is to build your own self-awareness and inner knowing. We would humbly suggest, with rare exceptions, that this should keep you busy for a while without concerning yourself too much with your children's personalities! What you can do is support your children in building their own self-awareness while you go about building yours. In Step Three of this book we will dive into the Nine Keys to unlocking your children's potential.

FIRST DAY
AT SCHOOL

1 "Listen to your teacher and do the right thing."

2 "Be kind to everyone and help the new kids who are a bit scared."

3 "Make lots of friends, sit at the front and sign up for everything."

4 "I will be thinking of you all day."

5 "Make sure you get all your information and the book list so we can get everything."

6 "Be careful and look after yourself."

7 "Have fun and enjoy yourself."

8 "Don't let anyone boss you around— stand up for yourself."

9 "Have a good day. Go with the flow and keep out of trouble."

Discover

Step Two:

Explore your parenting style

Now it's time to get curious. So far we have introduced you to the Enneagram and various concepts associated with it. We've also helped you work out your own Enneagram type, or at least two or three likely candidates.

In this step, you will explore the art of parenting *specifically as it relates to your type*. What follows are nine chapters – one dedicated to each Enneagram type. In each chapter we describe:

- how the type positively influences children
- how the type adversely affects children
- what is likely to cause stress to parents of this type
- what is likely to enhance the wellbeing of parents of this type
- tips and strategies that will support the growth of parents of this type.

We suggest you read the chapter about your own type first (or those on your shortlist – this may help you narrow the field). When you've had a chance to absorb that chapter, you might like to explore the others, perhaps starting with those related to your type's wings and arrows. You may start to see some of your own thought patterns and behaviours in those chapters. You may recognise, for instance, behaviours in your 'stress point' (the type connected by an arrow pointing away from yours) that tend to surface on those days when being a parent becomes particularly challenging. The tips in that chapter may then become relevant to you.

An important section in each of these chapters is headed 'Parenting strategies for growth'. There's a well-known saying that goes: "If you always do what you've always done, you'll always get what you've always got!" You have habits and coping strategies that you've used for years, and these will naturally be showing up in the way you parent. Change can be difficult, but in order to grow as a parent and enhance your relationship with

Explore

your children, you need to take the opportunity to experiment with different approaches. To begin with, the strategies and tips we offer may feel uncomfortable, even counterproductive, but practising them with patience and curiosity will help you improve your emotional intelligence and self-mastery – the greatest gift you can give to your children.

The Type One parent

The perfectionist and organiser

> **"The trouble with being punctual is that nobody**
> **is there to appreciate it"**
> **– F. P. Jones**

As parents, Ones are seeking a perfect world. They work diligently to improve themselves and teach their children responsibility and strong moral values. On the negative side, Ones can become highly critical and judgemental of themselves and others.

Strengths	Challenges
Productive	High expectations of self and others
Ordered	Inflexible and rigid
Strives for quality	Overly sensitive to criticism
Industrious	Perfectionistic
Self-disciplined	Critical of self and others
Crusader	Judgemental
Upholds justice	Obsessive compulsive
Honest and reliable	Overly serious
Clear and direct	Morally superior
Principled	Dogmatic
Ethical	Anxious

The Perfectionist
and Organiser

Type 1

How Ones influence their children

As a One, you strive for excellence and work hard at being a really good parent. You are raising your children in an environment that has a sense of honesty and integrity.

> *Shelley always tried her best at everything she did. It was important to her that her home was just right, that her kids were well mannered and kind and that her family presented as the perfect family. She would constantly follow her kids around, making sure they were doing the right thing and correcting them if she saw any mistakes, or even the potential for any mistakes. Shelley wanted her children to thrive and be successful in life, to demonstrate good values and to basically be good people. There was a fun side to Shelley as well. When she was able to relax and chill out a bit and not be so frenetic with making everything 'just so' she had a vibrant, even cheeky side to her that her children loved. They played all sorts of sports and games together and laughed so hard the children could forget about her often correcting them.*

How your type positively influences your children

The positive effects of your type as a parent include:

- As a conscientious moral leader, you instil family values of honesty, integrity and responsibility.
- Being consistent and fair, you set clear boundaries and can be relied upon by your family.
- Being good at putting facts together, you are able to come to clear understandings and figure out wise solutions to the family's challenges.
- You care deeply about being a good person, so you are a good role model to your children.
- You are focused on self-improvement, so you inspire your children to strive for excellence.
- You pay attention to detail, so your home is structured and orderly.

The Perfectionist and Organiser

Type 1

How your type adversely affects your children

Type One parents can become uptight and serious, always focusing on the faults of their children and constantly trying to improve them.

The potential negative effects of being a Type One parent include:

- You can have unrealistic expectations that are almost impossible for your children to meet. They either give up or feel inadequate for not being able to live up to your high standards.
- You get upset when you are not appreciated for what you do for others.
- You can get tense and anxious, and take things way too seriously.
- You can be very opinionated and impose your moral high ground onto your children.
- You can be rigid, have black-and-white thinking, and get stuck in a process or detail that inhibits your children's own free thinking.
- You don't like being criticised by others and may become defensive and critical of your family.

> *Shelley was consistent and fair and her children always knew where they stood and if she said something she meant it. One day Shelley told her children, "If you leave your things on the floor and they are not picked up before dinner I will collect everything that is left and put it in a box and give it to the poor people – no second chances!" And guess what? One of her kids, who was not great at following through, forgot to pick his things up. He lost them all to a charity. Shelley even made him go with her to the store and pass the things over so he would appreciate what he had (or didn't have) even more.*

What causes you stress as a parent

Being a parent can be stressful for everyone, but there are particular aspects of parenting that tend to increase the stress of Ones. These include:

The Perfectionist
and Organiser

Type 1

- feeling overburdened by a sense of too much personal responsibility
- seeing too many errors that need correcting
- not being able to quieten your inner critic
- your children being disobedient and dishonest
- others letting you down or not following through on what they say they will do
- others changing plans without consulting you
- mess or disorder in the home
- criticism of you or your family.

Shelley's need to have everything 'just right' backfired on her as well. As punishment for not bringing the car back when she asked, Shelley asked her son to wash and vacuum it. When she went out to check on his progress he was doing such a bad job that she said, "Oh this is hopeless and a very sub-standard job. I can't stand the errors you are making so just leave it and I will finish (read redo) the job". The son walked away with a big smile on his face, knowing that he had cunningly got out of doing a very boring task.

Type One variations

Arrows

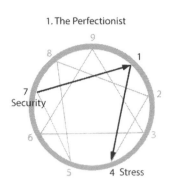

1. The Perfectionist

As we described in Step One, the arrows on the Enneagram give an indication of how – under certain circumstances – our behaviour can change from what is usual for our primary type. Under strain we move towards our 'stress point' and when relaxed we draw on the resources from our 'security point'.

Typically, when a Type One is under stress they will take on the negative aspects of a Type Four, and when feeling safe and secure they will take on the positive aspects of a Type Seven. We suggest you read the list at the beginning of the Type Four and Type Seven chapters in this section, describing strengths and challenges, to explore more about your stress and security points.

Wings

As with all types, the number on either side of your core type can influence and 'flavour' your behaviour. We call these your wings.

Type One parents tend to vary in their personalities depending on their dominant 'wing':

- Type Ones with a more developed Two wing tend to be a little more extroverted with their moral values in a public forum. On one hand they would like to please and be more helpful, but on the downside they may also be more critical and controlling.
- Type Ones with a more developed Nine wing tend to be more introverted, more philosophical, relaxed and objective; they would rather write about than preach their values. On the downside they may also be cooler and more detached.

What will enhance your self-mastery

As a Type One there are things you can practise that will help break down less resourceful habits and increase your self-mastery. As you stay present to these habits you become more aware and will be able to make better choices in the ways that you respond. Ultimately this will benefit all your relationships.

- Appreciate that there is more than one right way.
- Accept imperfections in yourself and others.
- Practise forgiving yourself and letting go of judgements.
- Take time for yourself to do fun things that you enjoy.
- Be able to laugh at yourself.
- Learn to recognise and process your anger.

Parenting strategies for growth

As mentioned in the introduction to this section, this is perhaps the most important part of this chapter. Challenging yourself to practise some of the following tips and strategies will help you grow as a parent. We suggest that you try out a small number of these strategies initially. There is no need to follow them in order: start with the ones that seem to be the easiest. Try to build them into the way you communicate and interact with your children. Choose just one a week if you like, noticing what impact the change has on your relationship and interactions with your family.

1. **Suspend your judgement:** Replace *always* being right with being kind or close. Practise stating criticisms gently and carefully so that your children feel that you love them unconditionally.

2. **Be more flexible:** Try not to obsess over the details. Become less rigid and allow for more spontaneity and freedom. Start to allow your children freedom to make their own choices and support them where possible.

3. **Be more accepting:** Be aware that you may appear self-righteous or morally superior to others. Your desire to improve others can feel like harsh criticism to your children. Not everyone sees the world from such a moral high ground. Learn to allow space for your children to grow into their own best self – whatever that may be. Practise asking them for their opinions and encourage discussion about different views.

4. **Practise being imperfect:** Your expectations may be set very high and your children could feel like a failure in your eyes when you show your disappointment. Learn to praise their efforts even if they do not meet your lofty standards. Practise showing your children that you do make the occasional mistake!

Type 1

5. **Express your anger calmly:** Feeling angry is okay. Learn to feel your anger without suppressing it or justifying it. Practise talking openly and calmly about why you feel angry, in a way that does not blame your children or undermine their self-esteem and confidence.

6. **Give yourself permission to have more fun:** Be less serious and intense and show your great sense of humour so that your kids can experience your lighter, fun side.

The Type Two parent

The helper and giver

Type 2

> **"I love you no matter what you do,**
> **but do you have to do so much of it?"**
> **— Jean Illsley Clarke**

As parents, Type Twos are very warm and encouraging; they listen well and are playful. At times, however, they can become overly concerned, worrying too much about everyone else's needs.

Strengths	Challenges
Helping	People pleasing
Loving	Possessive
Caring	Manipulative
Generous	Jealous
Encouraging	Overly intimate and intrusive
Enthusiastic	Patronising
Adaptable	Indirect
Compassionate	Proud of being needed
Sympathetic	Martyr like
Nurturing	Overly complimentary
Thoughtful	Thin skinned

The Helper
and Giver

Type 2

How Twos influence their children

Here's your favourite.

As a Type Two parent you are warm, loving and supportive of your children. You are aware of their real needs – they feel special and loved.

> *Jennifer prided herself on being generous, being there for others and going out of her way to love and support people. When it came to parenting, she enjoyed being a mum, particularly when the children were young, because she knew they needed her for so much and she was only too willing to give it to them. Jennifer seemed to always know what her children needed, even before they asked, and she made sure she met those needs for them. She seemed to get energy doing things for her family and enjoyed hearing every detail about their days at school.*

Type 2

How your type positively influences your children

Hello?

The positive effects of a Type Two parent include:

- Your love, nurture and support can give your children a sense of belonging and safety.
- You are sociable, friendly and approachable, which rubs off on your children.
- You have a good sense of humour and enjoy having fun with the whole family.
- You are naturally giving and helpful towards others and encourage these values in your children.
- You encourage your children, which helps raise their self-esteem.
- You have an intuitive sense for what your children feel and need.
- You are a good listener who can listen with your heart and be non-judgemental.

The Helper
and Giver

How your type adversely affects your children

The potential negative effects of being a Type Two parent include:

- You can be over protective and patronising, which will lead to your children being dependent on you.
- You may get anxious at times because you don't know how to relate to your children except through helping.
- Your desire to always be helpful can feel to others like you are taking over and manipulating them.
- You can get out of touch with your own needs and may become depleted emotionally and physically and then have little energy left for your family.
- You have difficulty expressing negative feelings such as anger and disappointment and confronting things you don't like: your children could get confused about what you are really feeling.
- You become insincere when you manipulate your children to like you by being overly flattering.
- When you feel unappreciated you can project guilt onto your family.

Type 2

> " *The kindergarten teacher of Jennifer's daughter, Becky, suggested to Jennifer that she did too much for her girl, and that this was preventing Becky from developing the necessary skills for life. Jennifer was shocked and a little indignant at the time. For a while she tried to step back and allow Becky to muddle through things herself, but before long it was just easier to do things for her rather than watch Becky struggle. A real challenge for Jennifer was when Becky said, "I can do it for myself". Jennifer felt frightened that she would no longer have a role to play in her daughter's life and found herself trying even harder to help Becky.* "

What causes you stress as a parent

Being a parent can be stressful for everyone, but there are particular aspects of parenting that tend to increase the stress of Twos. These include:

The Helper
and Giver

Type 2

- when your children don't want your help
- feeling unappreciated and uncared for when you know you have done so much for others
- times when you feel ignored and not valued
- worrying about what others are thinking of you
- avoiding disciplining your children because you're afraid they won't like you
- overextending yourself by always helping others
- being taken for granted.

Jennifer got very hurt when her son Harry, at 16 years of age, told her that he wanted her to back off and not get so involved in his life. She felt she was only showing interest and doing things for her children that they couldn't do for themselves. She felt so much a part of their lives and had spent countless hours and loads of energy helping them achieve their goals. Who was she if she couldn't help them? Jennifer tried to back off but no matter how often she tried she would always end up becoming as involved in their lives as ever.

As the children got older, Jennifer was still doing everything for them. She still made their breakfast and lunches and cooked every evening meal. She tidied their rooms, did their washing and ironing and drove them everywhere. At times she would feel exhausted but would not admit she needed any help, even to herself. It was her job to meet the needs of those around her and it was selfish to spend time looking after herself.

Type 2

Type Two variations

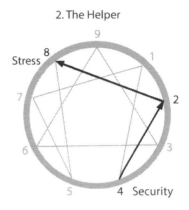

2. The Helper

Arrows

As we described in Step One, the arrows on the Enneagram give an indication of how – under certain circumstances – our behaviour can change from what is usual for our primary type. Under strain we move towards our 'stress point' and when relaxed we draw on the resources from our 'security point'.

Typically, when a Type Two is under stress they will take on the negative aspects of a Type Eight and when feeling safe and secure they will take on the positive aspects of a Type Four. We suggest you read the list at the beginning of the Type Four and Type Eight chapters, describing strengths and challenges, to explore more about your stress and security points.

Wings

As with all types, the number on either side of your core type can influence and 'flavour' your behaviour. We call these your wings.

Type Two parents tend to vary in their personalities depending on their dominant 'wing':

Type 2

- Twos with a stronger One wing tend to be more service oriented, idealistic and objective. However, the downside is you may become over involved in trying to be 'good'. You can be self-critical and judgemental, needing validation around giving and goodness.
- Twos with a stronger Three wing tend to be more success driven, self-assured, and image oriented. On the downside your ambition can lead to being overly direct and competitive.

> *"Never believe that a few caring people can't change the world. For, indeed, that's all who ever have* – Margaret Mead

What will enhance your self-mastery

As a Type Two there are things you can practise that will help break down less resourceful habits and increase your self-mastery. As you stay present to these habits you become more aware and will be able to make better choices in the ways that you respond. Ultimately this will benefit all your relationships.

Type 2

- Acknowledge your own needs and consciously take care of yourself.
- Notice when you intrude into your children's lives because you think you know what they need.
- Allow your children to go through some painful experiences without trying to rescue them.
- Encourage your children's independence.
- Develop your own interests so that you can detach from your children's lives.
- Be more assertive and direct about your own needs.

Parenting strategies for growth

As mentioned in the introduction to this section, this is perhaps the most important part of this chapter. Challenging yourself to practise some of the following tips and strategies will help you grow as a parent. We suggest that you try out a small number of these strategies initially. There is no need to follow them in order: start with the ones that seem the easiest. Try to build them into the way you communicate and interact with your children. Choose just one a week if you like, noticing what impact the change has on your relationship and interactions with your family.

1. **Get in touch with your own needs:** Notice your needs, wants and feelings. Developing your self-care without feeling guilty about putting yourself first will enhance your parenting. Your ability to help others will be more effective because you will not become exhausted and

The Helper
and Giver

Type 2

burnt out. Practise telling members of your family what you need and how you feel.

2. **Encourage your children's independence:** Allow them to look after themselves more. Practise waiting to be asked for help, rather than assuming your children need your assistance before they request it.

3. **Support, not rescue:** Recognise that there is a difference between support and rescue. It is good to offer support when a child is experiencing something difficult. However, trying to rescue them from reality robs them of the potential to develop their own coping strategies. Ask them what kind of support they require (and not necessarily from you).

4. **Find something you really enjoy doing:** Look for interests of your own that don't involve helping your family and other people. Recognise that your self-worth can come from other places besides helping others.

Type 2

5. **Create boundaries:** Be aware of being too permissive and avoiding setting boundaries and consequences for your children. Guard against becoming a people pleaser. It is okay to have some confrontation: your children will still love you if you use some discipline.

6. **Explore the intent of your giving:** Notice when you only help those who show their appreciation and make you feel good about yourself. Also notice when you feel resentful against those who don't. There can be a tendency for Type Two parents to make their children feel guilty for not appreciating or loving them enough. Learn to give without needing to get.

7. **Beware of flattery:** Become aware of how you use compliments. Do you ever use them to manipulate others into liking you? Do you seduce your family with flattery to win them over and get them to go along with you? Practise being truly authentic: be upfront and sincere about what it is you really want.

The Type Three parent

The achiever and motivator

Type 3

> *"The toughest thing about success is that you've got to keep on being successful" — Irving Berlin*

As parents, Threes are busy and organised. They encourage their family members to be goal orientated and active. On the negative side, they can become over-controlling and impatient, putting too much focus on achievement.

Strengths	Challenges
Confident	Intimidating
Organised	Inflexible
Efficient	Workaholic
Competent	Critical of others
Optimistic	Inauthentic
Energetic	Impatient
Goal orientated	Judgemental
Motivated	Overly competitive
Driven	Holding high expectations (of self and others)
Results focused	Overly image conscious
Productive	Narcissistic

How Threes influence their children

As a Type Three parent, your children see you as dependable. They know that things happen when you're around. You'll encourage them to make full use of their potential.

Carl was such an active hands-on dad: practical, organised and very involved in his children's lives. He had five children, and he would have loved more. Carl's friends were always amazed at how much time he found to juggle work and family life: he had a demanding job but was also the coach for his son's soccer team, a representative on the school P&C, he organised educational family trips at the weekend, and he scheduled everyone's sporting and fitness activities – of which there were plenty. He simply loved doing things with his family. Nothing satisfied him more than an action-packed weekend, and probably a few sports wins along the way!

How your type positively influences your children

The positive effects of a Type Three parent include:

- You motivate your family to focus and get things done – which can be useful for children who might procrastinate.
- You have energy and the ability to multitask; your family diary is organised and action packed, which can be fun and stimulating.
- You are reliable and loyal, which is very reassuring to your children.
- You are optimistic, friendly and upbeat, demonstrating resilience to your children.

- You are very flexible and adaptable, which helps your children become more resourceful.
- You are confident and can relate to many types of people. This helps your children develop adaptability.
- You have a friendly, competitive nature that encourages your family to succeed and be their best.

Type 3

It was rare that Carl's family would be doing nothing or wasting time. It was important to him that the family were productive; he didn't think well of other families who watched too much television or allowed their kids to laze around. One of his children felt irritated by this and complained that he pushed her too hard and expected too much. "We were rarely allowed to just chill and slob out – unless we were sick."

Carl was pleased with how he helped his children to set goals and how he motivated them to work hard and efficiently to achieve them. He felt glowing pride in what his children accomplished and achieved, it was hugely rewarding to him that his family had many successes to enjoy in their lives. He liked sharing stories with other parents about how competent his kids were, how much fun they had and how they were being their best. He enjoyed posting pictures on social media of his children's accomplishments and activities and how much they did.

75

Type 3

How your type adversely affects your children

Type Three parents have a tendency to over-organise their children in the pursuit of getting things achieved. You can easily become frustrated with your children's inefficiency and lack of responsibility.

Other potential adverse effects of being a Type Three parent include:

- You may set unrealistically high expectations for your children.
- You can be so focused on doing and achieving that you rush around and don't truly listen to your children – to them this can feel like you've dismissed them. When your mind is in multitask mode you are less likely to be giving your children the attention they need.

- You can come across as being abrupt.
- You get tired from doing so much – and then lack the energy to enjoy being with your kids.
- You can become impatient when your children don't do things as efficiently as you want them to.
- You may be judgemental of your children if you can't accept that they have their own way of doing things. This can be harmful to their self-esteem.
- You strive to avoid negative situations and failure, but in doing so you may miss opportunities to help your children learn from their mistakes.

During his children's teenage years, Carl grew impatient with one of his sons, who lacked ambition and drive. His son was a talented basketball player but chose not to try out for the team and wouldn't listen to his dad's well-intended advice and motivation. This frustrated Carl because he thought his son was being indecisive and lazy and was not interested in reaching his full potential. When Carl did slow down he was able to recharge his energy and enjoy just hanging out and being with his family rather than always being active with them. Secretly his family liked when Carl had a sports injury or was sick, because he stopped rushing around and they in turn could relax and just be.

Type 3

What causes you stress as a parent

Being a parent can be stressful for everyone, but there are particular aspects of parenting that tend to increase the stress of Threes. These include:

- when you see other parents parenting better than you
- when your children ignore your well-intentioned advice on how to do something efficiently
- when your children procrastinate or take too long to do something or make a decision
- not being acknowledged for the great things you do as a parent
- when you see your children not putting in the effort you think is needed for them to reach their potential

- believing that it's always you who has to "do something around here" – the rest of the family don't pull their weight as much as you do
- when you're so busy with work or a volunteer project that you don't have enough time left for your family
- when someone tells you to slow down.

Type Three variations

Arrows

As we described in Step One, the arrows on the Enneagram give an indication of how – under certain circumstances – our behaviour can change from what is usual for our primary type. Under strain we move towards our 'stress point' and when relaxed we draw on the resources from our 'security point'.

3. The Achiever

Typically, when a Type Three is under stress they will take on the negative aspects of Type Nine and when feeling safe and secure they will take on the positive aspects of a Type Six. We suggest you read the list at the beginning of the Type Six and Type Nine chapters, describing strengths and challenges, to explore more about your stress and security points.

Type 3

Wings

As with all types, the number on either side of your core type can influence and 'flavour' your behaviour. We call these your wings.

Type Three parents tend to vary in their personalities, depending on their dominant 'wing':

- Type Threes with a more developed Two wing tend to be warmer, more encouraging and sociable. On the downside, their desire to be popular and impress others can become a preoccupation. They can be seductive and covertly highly competitive.
- Type Threes with a more developed Four wing tend to be more introspective, sensitive, artistic, diplomatic and charming. On the downside side, they can be rather private socially and appear pretentious and arrogant.

What will enhance your self-mastery

As a Type Three there are things you can practise that will help break down less resourceful habits and increase your self-mastery. As you stay present to these habits you become more aware and will be able to make better choices in the ways that you respond. Ultimately this will benefit all your relationships.

- Slow down and take time to breathe.
- Let go of the outcome and focus on the present moment.
- Concentrate on listening without trying to fix or solve.
- Validate your children by appreciating that your way is not the only way.
- Stop thinking that you have to have it all.
- Remind yourself that you're a human *being* not a human *doing*.

Type 3

"Life moves pretty fast. If you don't stop and look around once in a while, you could miss it" – Ferris Bueller

Type 3

Parenting strategies for growth

As mentioned in the introduction to this section, this is perhaps the most important part of this chapter. Challenging yourself to practise some of the following tips and strategies will help you grow as a parent. We suggest that you try out a small number of these strategies initially. There is no need to follow them in order: start with the ones that seem the easiest. Try to build them into the way you communicate and interact with your children. Choose just one a week if you like, noticing what impact the change has on your relationship and interactions with your family.

1. **Share your feelings:** Start to acknowledge and share your feelings more with your family. Tell your children when you feel worried, tired, embarrassed, regretful, etc. You'll be showing them the human side that sits underneath your task-focused 'doing' side. This will connect you together at a deeper and more authentic level – it will make you more approachable.

2. **Respect their qualities:** Learn to really value and respect your children for *who they are* and not *what they do*. Spend some time thinking about what qualities you admire and respect in each of your children; for example, their patience, their empathy, their persistence, etc. Find new ways of telling them that you love and respect them for those qualities. You may have a tendency to focus on what they achieve, so be alert to what it is you are praising them for.

82

3. **The inner driver:** Become more aware of the internal dialogue driving you to keep busy. When you catch yourself being hectic or telling your children you can't be with them, take a moment to pause … Ask yourself what you will gain by completing that task right now, and what you will lose or sacrifice. Breathe, and ask yourself whether there might be a different way.

4. **Be discerning with your pace:** Learn how to flex your pace to match your children's when they need you to. To do this you'll need to switch off your multitasking capability and replace it with selective attention to the one thing your child needs at a given time. For example, when a child requests help with some homework,

try to switch off your mental list of other things that need doing. Focus selectively on them and avoid the temptation to multitask at the same time (cooking, checking email, folding laundry, watching the news). Your children will know when they haven't got your full attention.

5. **Be aware of your chameleon nature:** Keeping up appearances can be harmful and exhausting – and does not encourage you or your child to be authentic. Notice how you seek approval and accept that you can be loved and admired for who you are rather than by how successful you and your children are.

6. **The importance of setbacks:** Make more conscious use of setbacks or failures by modelling a sense of humility and resilience to your children. Setbacks can be a greater teacher than success.

The Type Four parent

The creative and individualist

Type 4

> *"A person can stand almost anything except a*
> *succession of ordinary days"* – Goethe

Type Four parents want a unique connection with their children. They are warm and compassionate and encourage their children to get in touch with their feelings. However, their focus of attention can easily go to what is missing in their lives and they can become melancholy and sad.

Strengths	Challenges
Warm	Overly sensitive
Creative	Dramatic
Intuitive	Self-righteous
Introspective	Self-absorbed
Supportive	Moody
Sincere	Judgemental and critical of others
Passionate	Melancholic
Gentle	Emotionally needy
Expressive	Temperamental
Unique	Moralistic
Refined	Jealous

The Creative
and Individualist

How Fours influence their children

As a Type Four parent you help your children to discover who they really are by encouraging their autonomy. You stimulate them intellectually and cre-atively.

Type 4

When I had my own kids I found it nerve wracking having these small beings who completely depended on me. The first months were difficult. I had to be involved, had to be engaged constantly – there was no time to zone out and be alone with myself to think. I love my kids with all my being – an immensely strong emotion that gave me sleepless nights and sometimes threatened to overwhelm me. I wanted to give them all possible opportunities in life and was determined they would know love and understanding, empathy and imagination – I would definitely foster their imaginations and appreciation of the finer things in life. Plus I would absolutely not, under any circumstances, project my own mood swings and, at times, negativity on them.

When they started school I was very nervous. What if they didn't fit in and couldn't find friends, how would I handle that? I constantly referenced my own childhood and remembered vividly how lost and lonely I had felt at times (even though I had good friends), how I always seemed to think so much more deeply about things than anyone else. I remember not understanding my feelings as a child and I was, therefore, determined I would always be there for my children to help them understand themselves. I never wanted them to feel lost or misunderstood.

How your type positively influences your children

The positive effects of your type on your children include:

- Your creative mind expands your children's horizons and allows them to think expansively.
- Your deep sense of empathy allows you to show compassion for your children.
- You are in tune with feelings and you encourage your children to get in touch with theirs – they feel understood and a deep sense of connection.
- You are intuitive and have a sense of what's going on for your children – you have a deep appreciation of their world.
- You encourage an appreciation of beauty, refinement, elegance and uniqueness that develops your children's appreciation of the finer things in life.

The Creative
and Individualist

Type 4

> *I perceived my son as a beautiful, sensitive and unique soul, who was not appreciated by his peers, and as he grew up I saw more and more of myself in him. Determined that he would always feel understood, I would sit on the end of his bed every night and ask him how his day had gone and did he want to talk about anything. If he did share his thoughts with me I would spend the next day analysing what he had said. This went on for some time, with me thinking I was doing the very best for my son. Then one night when I had gotten myself comfortable for our nightly chat, my son turned to me and said, "Mum I know you really enjoy chatting to me and finding out how I'm feeling about stuff, but it's okay, you don't have to. I'm fine – I'm not you!"*
>
> *At first I felt rejected and unappreciated, but as I thought it through I realised I had been making an assumption that he would share the same needs and wants as me. And of course he didn't; he was his own person. He was right – he wasn't me.*

How your type adversely affects your children

The potential negative effects of being a Type Four parent include:

- You have a tendency to notice what's missing, which can cause you to withdraw from your family.
- You can hold onto resentment and bear grudges. This can make it difficult for you and your family to move on and be in the present.
- Your inconsistent mood swings and negative energy can be very draining for the rest of your family.
- A tendency to be jealous of others can distract you

and you may neglect being present for your family as a result.

- Sometimes within your own family you might feel isolated and different and this prevents a good connection.

- By comparing and feeling judged, you tend to notice what you think is wrong with your children. This can lead to them having a sense of inadequacy.

- Your predisposition to feeling unworthy and being over-sensitive can make it hard for your family to connect and show their love for you.

The Creative
and Individualist

> *My daughter was completely different: outgoing, chatty, fun loving. All the things that I perceived I wasn't. She didn't respond to deep and meaningful chats, and would exhaust me with her constant energy and need for action. I sometimes found it hard to relate to her – she didn't automatically see the mystique and beauty in things around her; she didn't appreciate all the classic books I tried to get her to read. She lived in the moment; she actually did stop and smell the roses! She was so opposite to me that I struggled to find the connection I felt was necessary to good parenting. It took me a good while to realise how much she could teach me.*
>
> *I have subsequently learned to appreciate everything my beautiful children are and will be. I have, through them, learned to value the immediacy of life, and have stepped back to allow them to each develop their own uniqueness. They will achieve great things, be they ordinary or extraordinary.*

Type 4

What causes you stress as a parent

Being a parent can be stressful for everyone, but there are particular aspects of parenting that tend to increase the stress of Fours. These include:

91

- when you feel envious of other parents who seem more connected with their children than you are
- when you perceive that your children misunderstand, reject or ignore you
- receiving upsetting news or hearing about events that upset you
- people and experiences that lack emotional depth
- feeling that there is something wrong with you
- being asked to do something contrary to your values.

Type Four variations

Arrows

As we described in Step One, the arrows on the Enneagram give an indication of how – under certain circumstances – our behaviour can change from what is usual for our primary type. Under strain we move towards our 'stress point' and when relaxed we draw on the resources from our 'security point'.

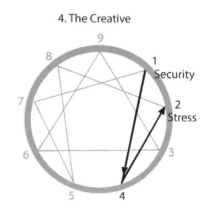

4. The Creative

Typically, when a Type Four is under stress they will take on the negative aspects of a Type One and when feeling safe and secure they will take on the positive aspects of a Type Two. We suggest you read the list

The Creative
and Individualist

at the beginning of the Type One and Type Two chapters, describing strengths and challenges, to explore more about your stress and security points.

Wings

As with all types, the number on either side of your core type can influence and 'flavour' your behaviour. We call these your wings.

Type Four parents tend to vary in their personalities, depending on their dominant 'wing':

Type 4

- Fours with a Three wing tend to be more extroverted, upbeat, ambitious and flamboyant. They love refinement, culture and sophistication. On the downside, they can be image conscious, competitive and disdainful of others.
- Fours with a Five wing tend to be more introverted, intellectual, idiosyncratic and reserved. Their real world is less interesting than the inner landscape they create for themselves. On the downside, they can be intensely private and depressed.

> *"It takes a genius to whine appealingly"*
> – F. Scott Fitzgerald

Type 4

What will enhance your self-mastery

As a Type Four there are things you can practise that will help break down less resourceful habits and increase your self-mastery. As you stay present to these habits you become more aware and will be able to make better choices in the ways that you respond. Ultimately this will benefit all your relationships.

- Notice when you feel validated, accepted and understood by your family.
- Focus on what is positive in your life.
- Stay the course, despite fluctuating moods and emotions.
- Be with people who use humour to lift and lighten your mood.
- Find a creative outlet.
- Get better at observing and accepting your emotions and not projecting them onto others.

- Achieve a healthy balance of sleep, work, exercise and diet.
- Be specific about your needs.

Parenting strategies for growth

As mentioned in the introduction to this section, this is perhaps the most important part of this chapter. Challenging yourself to practise some of the following tips and strategies will help you grow as a parent. We suggest that you try out a small number of these strategies initially. There is no need to follow them in order: start with the ones that seem the easiest. Try to build them into the way you communicate and interact with your children. Choose just one a week if you like, noticing what impact the change has on your relationship and interactions with your family.

Type 4

1. **Practise gratitude:** Recognise and appreciate the success and happiness of others. This will develop in you an inner sense of calm. Practise relaxing your self-judgement and focus on what is positive in your life right now.

2. **Be aware of avoiding the ordinary:** Practise appreciating what you have got and what you are doing rather than spending time thinking about what you could have, what you could be doing and what you wish you were doing. Your children might appreciate the ordinary things in their day; seek to understand what *they* want.

3. **Learn how to set boundaries:** You may be intense in your desire to build a deep and meaningful connection with your children. Relax your intensity and experiment with becoming more aware of when to step back and allow your child to have space.

4. **Focus on the task:** Practise focusing on the task at hand rather than indulging in the emotions that may be taking over in the present moment.

5. **Focus on the facts rather than the feelings:** Try to take an objective stance; do not over-rely on your feelings as the truth. Remind yourself of the facts and learn to distinguish facts from feelings. While you practise this, it might be helpful to write down facts and feelings.

6. **Practise appreciation:** Respect yourself and learn to appreciate your gifts and allow the positive side of your nature to emerge. Place more attention on your strengths and talents and less on comparing yourself with others. Your enhanced self-esteem will positively affect you and your family.

The Type Five parent

The observer and investigator

> **"Nothing in life is to be feared. It is only to be understood"**
> **— Marie Curie**

Type Five parents can be kind, perceptive, devoted and knowledgeable. They can also find it difficult to relate on an emotional level and may withdraw to have some quiet adult time.

Type 5

Strengths	Challenges
Love of learning	Emotionally withdrawn
Persevering	Aloof
Sensitive	Overly independent
Wise	Lacking spontaneity
Objective	Non-communicative
Perceptive	Stubborn
Self-contained	Critical of others
Analytical	Unassertive
Expert	Unemotional
Systematic	Secretive
Attentive	Intellectually arrogant

The Observer
and Investigator

How Fives influence their children

Type Five parents enjoy sharing their knowledge with their children and can be good at explaining difficult concepts. As a Five, you are good at looking at the big picture and can maintain a sense of perspective and objectivity in the home.

Type 5

> Steven had a long day at work. He was called into not one but two unscheduled meetings that went on and on. Worse still, there seemed to be no structure to them, yet at the end he was asked to state his position on the issues being discussed. Impossible, since he simply did not have enough facts at his disposal.
>
> As Steven drove home he was pleasantly thinking about having some time to himself to unwind. He only needed about an hour to process the day, write a few emails and then spend some time with the family.

How your type positively affects your children

The positive effects of your type on your children include:

- You are kind and devoted – your family can depend on your commitment to them.
- You can be grounded and keep things in perspective. You see the big picture for your family and don't get drawn into the drama.

- You have a brilliant mind and love learning for its own sake, and this encourages your children to have enquiring minds.
- You enjoy being wise and increasing your knowledge, and so can become a reliable resource for your children.

Type 5

The Observer
and Investigator

- You are self-sufficient and self-contained: you do not project your needs onto your children.
- You're very good at observing and can consider your responses without overreacting.

> When Steven arrives home it is bedlam. His wife is yelling at the kids, who are racing around the house, which looks like a bull has just run through it. His wife yells at him: "Thank God you're home. Can you please help the kids with their homework and get them into the bath while I tidy up and get dinner on".
>
> Steven stands there for a moment as a feeling of irritation comes up. He moves past his wife, heading to the study, letting her know he has important things to do and will be able to help in about 20 minutes.
>
> He goes to his office and is horrified to find that his desk has been tampered with and the kids have obviously been playing in there. However, the brief solitude calms him down a little and 15 minutes later he goes out to meet the 'mayhem'.

Type 5

How your type adversely affects your children

The potential negative effects of being a Type Five parent include:

- You can sometimes be authoritarian and demanding, responding with short bursts of temper.
- You can appear intellectually arrogant and your children may feel judged and intimidated.

Type 5

- You tend to avoid emotional attachment and your children may interpret this non-involvement as a lack of interest.
- You have difficulty sharing and showing your emotions. This makes it difficult for your children to learn emotional intelligence.
- You spend a lot of time in your head, thinking, and you may be slow to respond. You are busy formulating the most intelligent response, which hinders good, flowing conversation.
- Your need for privacy and space may turn you away from the typical parents' gatherings. Your children may miss opportunities.

The Observer
and Investigator

> *Beth is asking for help with her maths homework and Steven sits down and starts to explain the whys and wherefores of algebra before addressing the problem she is having trouble solving. She gets grumpy and says, "Come on Dad – enough of the history of maths. Just solve the problem for me." He is annoyed that all she wants him to do is give her the answer. Doesn't she realise how important it is to get a grasp on understanding it at a deeper level? Then it will all become clear and be easier with future maths problems.*
>
> *Steven is taking so long scribbling notes for Beth that she starts to tell him about her day and how horrible one of the girls at school was at recess and that she was very hurt and upset. He tunes out to her problems, as he doesn't want to get caught up in the minute details and drama of her girlfriends – it is way too much emotional information.*

What causes you stress as a parent

Being a parent can be stressful for everyone, but there are particular aspects of parenting that tend to increase the stress of Fives. These include:

- being unable to maintain sufficient privacy
- imposition on your personal boundaries and being interrupted
- being with people you don't want to be with (which you find tiring)
- trying to learn everything there is to know before taking action
- being exposed to excessive emotion from others and being unable to detach
- your children talking to others about your private family life
- feeling unable to control a situation
- being challenged on your ideas and knowledge.

Type Five variations

Arrows

As we described in Step One, the arrows on the Enneagram give an indication of how – under certain circumstances – our behaviour can change from what is usual for our primary type. Under strain we move towards our 'stress point' and when relaxed we draw on the resources from our 'security point'.

5. The Observer

Typically, when a Type Five is under stress they will take

on the negative aspects of a Type Seven and when feeling safe and secure they will take on the positive aspects of a Type Eight. We suggest you read the list at the beginning of the Type Seven and Type Eight chapters, describing strengths and challenges, to explore more about your stress and security points.

Wings

As with all types, the number on either side of your core type can influence and 'flavour' your behaviour. We call these your wings.

Type Five parents tend to vary in their personalities, depending on their dominant 'wing':

- Fives with a more developed Four wing tend to be more creative, humanistic, sensitive and empathetic. They often use the imagination more than the analytical part of their mind. On the downside, they can become more self-absorbed and have difficulty staying grounded.

- Fives with a more developed Six wing tend to be more loyal, co-operative and disciplined. They are more interested in practical matters, facts and details than the other wing combination. On the downside, they are more detached, sceptical and cautious. They may be more aggressive and actively antagonise people who disagree with them.

Type 5

> *"I know that I am intelligent, because I know*
> *that I know nothing"* – Socrates

What will enhance your self-mastery

Type 5

> Nice, dad. Use your instep!

As a Type Five there are things you can practise that will help break down less resourceful habits and increase your self-mastery. As you stay present to these habits you become more aware and will be able to make better choices in the ways that you respond. Ultimately this will benefit all your relationships.

- Become more assertive and outspoken.
- Relax your need to know it all.

The Observer
and Investigator

- Become more physically active and engaged with your children.
- Lighten up and have fun with your family.
- Become a more active listener.
- Talk more about your feelings.

Parenting strategies for growth

As mentioned in the introduction to this section, this is perhaps the most important part of this chapter. Challenging yourself to practise some of the following tips and strategies will help you grow as a parent. We suggest that you try out a small number of these strategies initially. There is no need to follow them in order: start with the ones that seem easiest. Try to build them into the way you communicate and interact with your children. Choose just one a week if you like, noticing what impact the change has on your relationship and interactions with your family.

1. **Express your emotions:** Allow yourself to experience feelings instead of detaching and retreating into your mind and room. Be aware that you tend to share very little of yourself, which can create a barrier between you and your family. Practise actively engaging more with your family.

2. **Practise small talk:** Find ways to engage in conversation and practise staying present during what you perceive as the boring chit-chat of your children. Show interest in what may seem like mundane conversation

Type 5

107

– it is very important for your children to be seen and heard by you.

3. **Practise not needing to know:** Be careful about being too analytical and concentrating only on the facts. Trust your instinct. During your information gathering you might miss out on what is really important to your children and they may feel talked at. Real life emerges between the lines – practise listening to them without needing to know, join the dots or make sense of their stories.

4. **Expand your social skills:** Place importance on developing your social skills. Your children may need you to interact with others on their behalf, and your behaviour will model social interaction for them.

The Observer
and Investigator

5. **Become more physically active:** Get out of your head and into your body. Be aware of when you are over-thinking, as thinking can often replace doing. You will become more open, approachable and engaging with your family.

6. **Be aware of your energy management:** You have a higher requirement for time and space alone in order to recharge. Be open and honest about this need so that your family docsn't fccl likc you are avoiding them. However, notice when you are using this detachment as an excuse to withdraw inappropriately.

Type 5

The Type Six parent

The questioner and loyalist

> **"An ounce of loyalty is worth a pound of cleverness"**
> **– Elbert Hubbard**

Type Six parents can show up in two different ways. They can be very loving and devoted to their children, with a strong sense of loyalty and humour. However, some Sixes are constantly scanning for danger, fearing the worst-case scenario, which can develop anxiety in their children. Others confront their fears and can become overly assertive, which can overwhelm their children. Both these characteristics can appear in the same person.

Type 6

Strengths	Challenges
Loyal	Anxious and fearful
Cautious	Hyper-vigilant
Responsible	Defensive
Charming and witty	Suspicious
Curious	Rule follower or challenger
Protects the underdog	Authoritarian but also struggles with authority issues
Trustworthy and honourable	Indecisive, which leads to procrastination
Well prepared	Controlling and rigid
Helpful	Doubts self and others
Honours commitments	Stubborn
Caring	Unpredictable

How Sixes influence their children

As a Type Six parent, your children can sense your loyalty and solidness and they feel secure and protected. Your wit and charm can bring a light-heartedness into the family.

Type 6

James had a great sense of humour and could be a bit of a clown. His kids loved it when they had friends around and Dad cracked a few jokes with them. James also looked out for the kids who seemed a bit on the outer and made a point of talking to them and including them in the fun.

How your type positively influences your children

The positive effects of Sixes as parents include:

- You are a loyal and reliable parent, which can give your children a sense of security.
- You prepare for every scenario. Your children will feel safe and cared for.
- You have a sense of humour and wit, which can be fun for the whole family.
- You are warm and compassionate, and this creates a sense of genuine care for your family.
- You are protective – you are always ready to fight for the underdog.
- You give attention to detail – you will stick at a task and the family will know that it will be done well.

Type 6

The Questioner
and Loyalist

James was looking forward to taking his family on a camping trip to Central Australia. He wanted to make sure it was a wonderful and safe holiday, so he made sure that he prepared thoroughly for every contingency. He wanted to keep his family comfortable as well as giving them a great adventure.

He had purchased a new 4WD for some outback driving and decided it would be best to have some extra spare parts for the engine. He did not want the family to be stranded on some outback track. He also decided to get an extra water tank for the camper van and an extra battery for the 4WD, just in case.

As he would be travelling in unfamiliar and remote territory, James also took several maps and a satellite phone. The thought of them getting lost, the car breaking down, or someone being unwell or injured without sufficient communication was a real concern for him. It made him feel quite anxious. However, by being prepared, he knew he would feel more confident and his anxiety would ease.

Packing up required a great deal of thought. One could never be certain of the weather, so he made sure everyone in the family packed enough clothes for the heat, the cold and the wet.

Even though the rest of the family teased James for all his planning and attention to detail, they felt secure knowing that he had thought of everything they might need, in any situation, and they always knew that he would look after them.

Type 6

How your type adversely affects your children

The potential negative effects of being a Type Six parent include:

- Your constant anxiety for the safety of your children can become smothering. Your children may then become rebellious in their teenage years.
- You often project your fears onto your children who may grow up becoming fearful and lacking in confidence themselves.
- You can procrastinate trying to make up your mind and end up going round in circles. This can be frustrating for the family.
- You don't trust your own authority but keep checking to see what others think. However, you also doubt what others say and can then appear over-authoritarian and confrontational because you are feeling unsure of yourself.
- You can become overly dutiful and bound by rules

Type 6

and regulations, which can feel very restrictive to your children.

- Your fear and questioning mind can cause you to project your fears, unrealistically, onto your children.
- Your children can find your constant anxiety quite stifling.

> *The night before they left on their camping trip, James felt very anxious. He wondered if he was doing the right thing taking his family to such remote places. What if one of them got a snakebite or took ill and they were far from anywhere? What if they had an accident? What if there was a flood, or they ran out of water or petrol? As he thought of all these possibilities, his anxiety increased. His hyper-vigilance could make everyone around him feel stressed.*

What causes you stress as a parent

Being a parent can be stressful for everyone, but there are particular aspects of parenting that tend to increase the stress of Sixes. These include:

Type 6

- your need for certainty, which causes you to feel anxious much of the time
- feelings that you can't trust your children or anyone else
- seeing your children bullied or taken advantage of
- thinking that your children are not giving you the loyalty and respect you deserve
- questioning your own authority
- trying to decide how to discipline your children
- getting busier and busier.

Type 6

James worried constantly about his children and often thought of all the dangers and challenges they faced every day. His underlying anxiety tended to bring a heaviness with it. He knew he questioned everyone a bit too much, yet he seldom seemed to get the assurance he needed to feel that everything was okay. He wanted his children to think things through logically and often questioned their thinking and ideas. His sceptical attitude could make them feel undermined and he wondered why they didn't want to engage with him at times.

The Questioner
and Loyalist

Type Six variations

Arrows

6. The Questioner

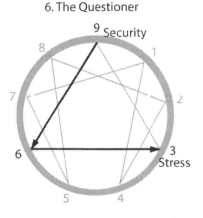

As we described in Step One, the arrows on the Enneagram give an indication of how – under certain circumstances – our behaviour can change from what is usual for our primary type. Under strain we move towards our 'stress point' and when relaxed we draw on the resources from our 'security point'.

Typically, when a Type Six is under stress they will take on the negative aspects of a Type Three and when feeling safe and secure they will take on the positive aspects of a Type Nine. We suggest you read the list at the beginning of the Type Three and Type Nine chapters, describing strengths and challenges, to explore more about your stress and security points.

Type 6

Wings

As with all types, the number on either side of your core type can influence and 'flavour' your behaviour. We call these your wings.

Type Six parents tend to vary in their personalities, depending on their dominant 'wing':

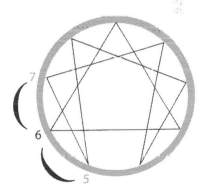

119

- Sixes with a more developed Five wing tend to be more introverted, intellectual and cautious. They are systems people and thorough researchers. On the downside, they can be cynical, stand-offish and isolate themselves .
- Sixes with a more developed Seven wing tend to be more extroverted, materialistic and relationship oriented. They often combine energy, humour and a zest for life. On the downside, they can be insecure and have problems with procrastination.

> *"I like pessimists. They're always the ones who bring lifejackets for the boat"* — Lisa Kleypas

Type 6

What will enhance your self-mastery

As a Type Six there are things you can practise that will help break down less resourceful habits and increase your

The Questioner
and Loyalist

self-mastery. As you stay present to these habits you become more aware and will be able to make better choices in the ways that you respond. Ultimately this will benefit all your relationships.

- Loosen up a little and have more fun with your family.
- Step back from your children's lives and allow them to fight their own battles.
- Recognise your own inner authority and trust your own decisions.
- Look more on the positive side of life.
- Recognise that rules and regulations are often guide-lines and not necessarily absolute.

Parenting strategies for growth

As mentioned in the introduction to this section, this is perhaps the most important part of this chapter. Challenging yourself to practise some of the following tips and strategies will help you grow as a parent. We suggest that you try out a small number of these strategies initially. There is no need to follow them in order: start with the ones that seem easiest. Try to build them into the way you communicate and interact with your children. Choose just one a week if you like, noticing what impact the change has on your relationship and interactions with your family.

1. **Manage your stress levels:** You tend to overthink things. Learn different ways to help relieve your anxiety, such as meditation, breathing techniques and being out in nature. As you learn to manage your

Type 6

stress levels, the whole family will feel more relaxed. Experiment with some new ways to relax and chill out.

2. **Learn to trust your own inner authority:** Notice when you make a decision based on what others say because you think everyone else knows better than you do. Practise asking yourself, "What do I think/ want to do about this issue?" You usually have some very sound insights.

3. **Develop a realistic belief:** Find the courage to accept responsibility for the decisions you make. It is okay to make mistakes as long as you learn from them. Your children will also learn that it is not the end of the world if you or they make mistakes.

Type 6

4. **Learn to trust your children:** Practise releasing the tight grip you have on your children because you are fearful for their safety and wellbeing. They need to feel they can be trusted to look after themselves. Practise allowing them to take some risks.

5. **Loyalty:** Be aware when your loyalty is blinding you to the reality of a situation – it may be destructive to your own wellbeing and that of your family. Practise becoming more curious about when you might be overplaying your quality of loyalty – start to ask yourself more questions.

6. **Become less rigid:** Allow your children to see there is some wriggle room around your family guidelines. It is more about the spirit of the law, rather than the letter of the law. Be careful where you direct your anger. Notice how being intimidating masks more vulnerable feelings. Build in some flexibility: you can have authority without being authoritarian.

Type 6

The Type Seven parent

The enthusiast and epicure

> ## *"If you obey all the rules you miss all the fun"*
> ## – Katharine Hepburn

Type Seven parents are full of energy and optimism for their family. They seek out fun things for their children to do; they enjoy being happy and playing. However, when this upbeat energy is overplayed the Seven parent can be overwhelming to their children, leaving them feeling neither seen nor heard.

Strengths	Challenges
Optimistic	Hyperactive
Spontaneous	Impulsive
Creative and imaginative	Unfocused
Enthusiastic	Flippant
High energy	Overindulgent
Confident	Intimidating
Highly productive	Overwhelmed and unproductive
Fun loving	Avoiding of pain and discomfort
Open minded	Narcissistic
Positive thinking	Rebellious
Quick	Restless

Type 7

The Enthusiast
and Epicure

How Sevens influence their children

To your children, you are upbeat and motivating. They will see you planning enjoyable activities, contributing to the world and having fun. This can be inspiring.

Let's do India next!

Ann always took everything in her stride: she was upbeat, enthusiastic, happy and always busy. When she became a parent she naturally threw her energy and excitement into building her family. When her children were young, Ann loved finding new and creative ways of enriching their lives. She arranged lots of play dates, craft sessions, theatre outings and adventures. Ann enjoyed playing, making up games, putting on little shows with her children. Birthdays were always celebrated with parties and social gatherings. It made her happy to plan the next new experience for them, yet there was always room for a spontaneous trip into the city or to the beach if Ann spotted something exciting that she wanted to show her children.

When her children felt sad or were having a bad day, Ann had a great knack of cheering them up. She could help them reframe tricky situations and she taught them how to see the positive side of life, which they relied on her for. As they grew into teenagers, Ann had to learn that sometimes they wanted to talk more about what they found upsetting or painful, and she had to resist the urge to immediately cheer them up and move them on.

Type 7

How your type positively influences your children

The positive effects of Type Seven parents include:

- You are a quick thinker – you help your children overcome challenges and keep moving forward.
- You are creative and imaginative – you add richness to your children's lives with storytelling and imaginative thinking.
- You have a love of life, encouraging your children to get out there and explore the world.
- You are optimistic and tend to focus on the positives. You encourage your family to look on the bright side of life.
- You find great opportunities for your children to discover life – you encourage (or even find) opportunities for them.

- You are friendly and outgoing, encouraging friendships and social interactions for your family.
- You are good at reframing – you are able to spin negatives and turn them into positives.

> *Because Ann wanted to keep her options open, she would often over-commit her family with too much activity, or sometimes she would not commit at all – just in case another more interesting thing came along. Ann didn't like to feel restricted; having many choices felt liberating and she wanted her children to grow up being flexible and enjoying great variety. As they got older, Ann would encourage her children to try and experiment with new activities, friends, places and experiences, and she really enjoyed talking with them about everything they did. Ann wanted to keep them open minded. Sometimes her family teased her about all the plans she had, and how quickly she'd drop them if she got bored and move onto something new. They also got frustrated when deadlines weren't met or the family didn't see something through to completion.*

Type 7

How your type adversely affects your children

Be aware that you have a tendency to avoid the less exciting and mundane things in life. Keeping things upbeat and positive can be exhausting for your family (and in the end for you too).

The potential negative effects of being a Type Seven parent include:

- You can be so busy looking for new things to do that you over-commit and run out of quality time for your family.
- You often run late or don't make commitments because you try to keep all your options open. Your children may see you as unreliable.
- Your fun-loving humour and spontaneity can come across as immature, and this sometimes embarrasses your children.
- Your egalitarian approach to authority can lead to unclear boundaries between parent and child.

Type 7

130

The Enthusiast
and Epicure

- You can be undisciplined and get bored with routine, which means important family tasks often don't get completed.
- Your impulsiveness and inconsistency can be confusing for your family.

> *What Ann found challenging in the early days of motherhood was the repetitiveness of parenting tasks associated with young children. She easily became bored with the routine and mundane stuff; it actually made her impatient at the time. Looking back now, Ann can see she missed out on enjoying some of the everyday moments.*
>
> *One of the things Ann felt weak about in her parenting was her ability to discipline her children. She avoided causing them too much pain, she didn't like conflict in the family at all and she tried to even out the authority. At times she doubted her style and worried that she didn't give her children tighter boundaries and consequences. But to Ann, the role of Mum wasn't about using hierarchy and being the 'boss', it was always about making everyone in the family feel equal and know that they belonged.*

What causes you stress as a parent

Being a parent can be stressful for everyone, but there are particular aspects of parenting that tend to increase the stress of Sevens. These include:

- seeing other families having more experiences and enjoyment than your own

Type 7

- feeling dismissed or not taken seriously
- feeling as if you have been unjustly criticised
- running out of time to do all the exciting things you have planned
- when your children are negative or sad or show a pessimistic attitude
- seeing your children wasting opportunities and turning things down
- making mistakes and getting things wrong
- feeling trapped by the mundane tasks and responsibilities of being a parent
- feeling that you *have* to do something and don't have a choice.

The Enthusiast
and Epicure

Type Seven variations

Arrows

As we described in Step One, the arrows on the Enneagram give an indication of how – under certain circumstances – our behaviour can change from what is usual for our primary type. Under strain we move towards our 'stress point' and when relaxed we draw on the resources from our 'security point'.

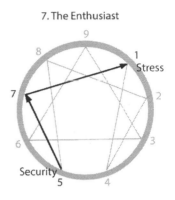

Typically, when a Type Seven is under stress they will take on the negative aspects of a Type One and when feeling safe and secure they will take on the positive aspects of a Type Five. We suggest you read the list at the beginning of the Type Five and Type One chapters, describing strengths and challenges, to explore more about your stress and security points.

Wings

As with all types, the number on either side of your core type can influence and 'flavour' your behaviour. We call these your wings.

Type Seven parents tend to vary in their personalities, depending on their dominant 'wing':

Type 7

- Sevens with a more developed Six wing tend to be more loyal, endearing, responsible and willing to compromise. They are curious, with an excellent sense of humour. On the downside, they may become anxious, lose focus and become scattered, with less follow-through than the other wing.
- Sevens with a more developed Eight wing tend to be more exuberant, realistic and independent. They think strategically and can quickly organise their resources. On the downside, they can be more aggressive, competitive and materialistic. Others may see Sevens as being outspoken and even a bit callous.

> *"Life is either a great adventure or nothing"*
> *– Helen Keller*

What will enhance your self-mastery

As a Type Seven there are things you can practise that will help break down less resourceful habits and increase your self-mastery. As you stay present to these habits you become more aware and will be able to make better choices in how you respond. Ultimately this will benefit all your relationships.

Type 7

The Enthusiast
and Epicure

- Practise saying "No" to taking on extra things.
- Focus on getting things completed before starting another task.
- Become aware of when you are exaggerating or being unrealistically optimistic.
- Listen and allow others to talk about their sadness or pain ... without positively reframing it for them.
- Appreciate what you have, rather than searching for something better.
- Allow your children to go at their own pace, not moving them on at your speed.

Type 7

135

Parenting strategies for growth

As mentioned in the introduction to this section, this is perhaps the most important part of this chapter. Challenging yourself to practise some of the following tips and strategies will help you grow as a parent. We suggest that you try out a small number of these strategies initially. There is no need to follow them in order: start with the ones that seem easiest. Try to build them into the way you communicate and interact with your children. Choose just one a week if you like, noticing what impact the change has on your relationship and interactions with your family.

1. **Check your upbeat energy:** Check that your upbeat energy isn't out of sync with your family's needs. Have discussions with your family about the activities and social engagements you participate in. Get everyone's views. Work on how you manage your disappointment if your family doesn't share your enthusiasm for more happiness, adventure, experience, etc.

2. **Be aware of your positive spin:** Become more aware of when you are putting a positive spin on what's really happening. Are you reframing reality? You are good at making the best of an awful situation – but in reframing the negative, are you denying or avoiding something? Practise listening to what your children don't like, or find painful or uncomfortable. It is important they see that life can be joy *and* sorrow. Learn to pass through these difficult situations more honestly.

The Enthusiast
and Epicure

3. **Practise being more persistent:** Learn to stay with a particular plan or activity for longer. Stick with things. Become more tenacious and bring family projects to a conclusion rather than giving up and trying something new or different.

4. **Respect everyone's differences:** Your children might have personality types that yearn for structure, and think in concrete detail. Learn that this is who they are. Where you see new ideas and change, they might prefer the security of repetition and stability. Learn to curb your impatience and appreciate what they find interesting.

5. **Notice your frenetic mind:** Become more aware of when your thoughts are racing ahead and becoming unfocused. Take time to stop, breathe and then focus your thoughts. Slow down, value your own space

Type 7

and down time, and become more centred so you can engage more effectively with your family.

6. **Resist the temptation to always cheer people up:** Be aware of your habit of avoiding painful situations and emotions. Be honest with your family about painful feelings. For your children it might be important to sit with pain and discomfort longer than you think necessary. By forcing them to move on, you may be robbing them of the opportunity to process these things.

Type 7

The Type Eight parent

The asserter and protector

Type 8

> ## *"The best way out of a problem is through it"*
> ## – Robert Frost

Type Eight parents are the strong protectors of their children. They are loyal, caring, involved and devoted. However, their intensity can also be overbearing for their family.

Strengths	Challenges
Energetic	Controlling
Courageous	Intimidating
Passionate	Demanding
Protective	Impatient
Supportive	Rebellious
Seeking justice	Sceptical
Direct	Insensitive
Empowering of others	Intolerant of weakness and disloyalty
Self-confident	Judgemental
Authoritative	Overbearing
Resourceful	Aggressive

Type 8

The Asserter
and Protector

How Eights influence their children

As an Eight parent, when you feel relaxed and in control your children feel your warmth and generosity. You are raising your children in an environment that has a sense of security and love.

Ben was a warm and generous parent. He was always at his kids' sporting events, often acting as coach, organising the team events and keeping everything running smoothly. He liked to take control of things and usually ended up becoming the club president. What he didn't know was that he had a nickname – the 'benevolent dictator' – as there was only one way to do things, and that was his way. Ben wasn't aware that sometimes in his desire to make things happen he could become very bossy, even intimidating. He felt good, as he was moving the club forward and taking it in a new direction that would ultimately be great, not only for the club, but for the local community as well.

Type 8

How your type positively influences your children

The positive effects of Type Eight parents include:

- You are a warm and generous parent – you can be encouraging for less self-assured children.
- Your sheer enjoyment of life can be contagious – your children will love your fun and energetic spirit.
- Your courage to try new things can be fun for the whole family, and they will feel secure to venture out with you.
- Your support creates a sense of warmth and connectedness and your children will feel the protectiveness.
- Your resourcefulness provides many opportunities for your children to explore, which will help expand their horizons.
- You have a strong sense of justice – you will empower your children to stand up for what is right.

Type 8

The Asserter
and Protector

When Ben was relaxed and calm he presented a side of himself that
not many people saw – his soft side. Ben thought that it was weak to
show that he was vulnerable and so he very rarely asked for help or
showed this softer side. One day when he was not well (which didn't
happen very often) he actually had to ask one of his sons for help to
get something finished. His son was very surprised but enjoyed being
able to help his dad.

Ben's enjoyment of life could be contagious. His kids loved his
adventurous and fun spirit and that they did some amazing things
together that many families didn't.

How your type adversely affects your children

The potential negative effects of being a Type Eight parent
include:

- When you become angry and intense, you can be
  overwhelming and frightening for your children.

Type 8

- When stressed you can get to the point of exhaustion and distance yourself from your family and become remote.
- You can be restless and impatient when your children 'just don't get it'.
- You can put a lot of pressure on yourself, which shortens your fuse and can cause you to explode.
- Type Eight mothers often have a hard time, as their strength and assertiveness can be misconstrued as aggression.
- You are not good at showing your vulnerability and as a result others perceive that you don't need their support.
- You expect your children to follow your rules, and you become angry and controlling if they don't.

Ben knew that one of his biggest faults was the occasional outburst of anger. He found it really hard to contain this anger as it flared up very quickly, especially when his kids broke rules or boundaries. He was worried that sometimes his kids looked scared and afraid when he blew his top. This was not how he wanted things to be.

Ben's two boys often bore the brunt of his stern behaviour, which was particularly tough for one son, as he was quite soft and gentle and all his father wanted was for him to toughen up so he wouldn't get hurt in this very tough world. Ben knew it was important to protect his sons, but he also wanted to empower them to stand up for themselves and what is right.

Type 8

What causes you stress as a parent

Being a parent can be stressful for everyone, but there are particular aspects of parenting that tend to increase the stress of Eights. These include:

- when your children ignore your well-intentioned guidelines and expectations
- trying to contain your energy and enthusiasm, especially when they are related to a cause you are passionate about
- when others attempt to control you or tell you what to do
- having to contain your confrontational style
- going full out and denying fatigue
- when your children are untruthful

Type 8

- believing you must be strong and powerful to ensure the protection of your children in a tough, unjust world
- denying your own fears, weaknesses and vulnerabilities.

Type Eight variations

Arrows

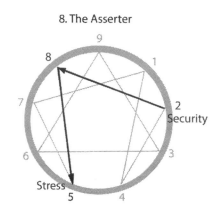

8. The Asserter

As we described in Step One, the arrows on the Enneagram give an indication of how – under certain circumstances – our behaviour can change from what is usual for our primary type. Under strain we move towards our 'stress point' and when relaxed we draw on the resources from our 'security point'.

Typically, when a Type Eight is under stress they will take on the negative aspects of a Type Five and when feeling safe and secure they will take on the positive aspects of a Type Two. We suggest you read the list at the beginning of the Type Two and Type Five chapters, describing strengths and challenges, to explore more about your stress and security points.

Type 8

146

The Asserter
and Protector

Wings

As with all types, the number on either side of your core type can influence and 'flavour' your behaviour. We call these your wings.

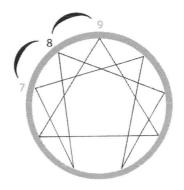

Type Eight parents tend to vary in their personalities, depending on their dominant 'wing':

- Eights with a more developed Seven wing tend to be more extroverted, enterprising, energetic and quick. They have energy to burn and love projects, exercise and ventures to burn off energy. On the downside, they are impulsive, impatient and egocentric. They are more openly aggressive and less likely to back down from a fight.

- Eights with a more developed Nine wing tend to be more mild mannered, gentle, receptive and quietly strong. They are not as openly aggressive, ready to be strong if needed and asserting power and leadership through protectiveness. On the downside, they can go back and forth between strength and ease, which can be hard for some people to read.

> *"If you've got them by the balls their hearts and minds will follow"*
> **– John Wayne**

Type 8

147

What will enhance your self-mastery

As a Type Eight there are things you can practise that will help break down less resourceful habits and increase your self-mastery. As you stay present to these habits you become more aware and will be able to make better choices in how you respond. Ultimately this will benefit all your relationships.

- Pause, slow down and cultivate patience.
- Notice your intensity and its impact and choose a gentler approach.
- Resist the urge to dismiss or invalidate another's point of view.
- Take the time to listen without fixing, solving or judging.
- Think things through more before acting.
- Open up to others and reveal your vulnerability.

Parenting strategies for growth

As mentioned in the introduction to this section, this is perhaps the most important part of this chapter. Challenging yourself to practise some of the following tips and strategies will help you grow as a parent. We suggest that you try out a small number of these strategies initially. There is no need to follow them in order: start with the ones that seem easiest. Try

Type 8

148

The Asserter
and Protector

to build them into the way you communicate and interact with your children. Choose just one a week if you like, noticing what impact the change has on your relationship and interactions with your family.

1. **Contain your energy:** When you are not so big in the space, you leave room for your children and partner to come forward and freely express themselves. Practise pulling back your energy a little – allow others to speak, to make recommendations, to lead and to make decisions.

2. **Be more open to listening and negotiating differences:** Making a conscious effort to 'tell' less and 'ask' more so your children can be encouraged to develop into their own unique personalities. Use questions to help your children develop an idea they have, for example, "That sounds an interesting plan – tell me more about how you see that working out" or "That sounds really important to you, tell me more ..."

3. **Learn to be less controlling:** Be more aware of blurring the line between control and protective empowerment. When you are too structured and controlling you push your children away. Practise relaxing a bit more and going with the flow.

4. **Be more tactful:** Learn how to be less direct so you are less hurtful. Often the first thing out of your mouth is a criticism or a blunt truth. Pause and create a space between what you are thinking and what you are saying so that you can choose words and a tone that are more encouraging.

Type 8

5. **Take responsibility for your anger:** You have a tendency to blame others for your anger. Pause, take a breath and re-examine what might be your part in a confrontation. Take a reality check on your own behaviour. Ask yourself what you could change.

6. **Consider others' points of view:** Be willing to listen to others without trying to convince them to agree with you. Make an effort to see ambiguity. Practise standing in their shoes – what does the world look like from their point of view?

7. **Learn to show your vulnerability:** You often feel that you must be superhuman. Remember: you can't be all and do all for everyone. Your children and your partner want to support you and be there for you, but if you don't show any vulnerability they will come to believe that you don't need that support. Vulnerability is uncertainty, risk and emotional exposure and there is great strength in being open and showing your true feelings. Practise expressing your authentic feelings – tell your loved ones when you feel worried, anxious or sad.

The Type Nine parent

The accommodator and peacekeeper

> **"Never put off till tomorrow what you can avoid altogether"**
> **– Preston's Axiom**

Type Nine parents are good listeners and mediators and can merge into the world of their children. They are easygoing and flexible, but can also be stubborn and overly permissive with their children.

Strengths	Challenges
Easygoing	Avoids conflict
Patient	Denies anger but explodes occasionally
Diplomatic	Procrastinates
Peaceful	Loses sense of self and blends with others
Good listener	Stubborn
Accepting of others	Complacent
Understanding of all points of view	Indecisive
Supportive	Disengaged
Encouraging	Appeasing
Generous	Unassertive
Steadfast	Low energy

Type 9

How Nines influence their children

As a Type Nine parent, when you are warm and easygoing your children will feel supported and comfortable in your presence.

Kerry felt that becoming a mother was the best thing she had ever done. She loved her children unconditionally and provided a safe and comfortable home for them. Because she was a good listener and didn't try to give too much advice, the children felt they could open up to her. She understood each one of them intuitively and was able to see every child's point of view.

Kerry was very proud of her children. She supported all their activities and felt energetic and motivated to help them achieve their goals. When they did, it felt like she had also achieved something

Type 9

How your type positively influences your children

The positive effects of a Type Nine parent include:

- Your warmth and understanding help your children feel accepted – they will feel your unconditional love.
- Your easygoing approach will have your children feeling relaxed and they will not feel unduly pressured by you.
- Your ability to mediate can help diffuse conflict, which will allow your children to appreciate other people's points of view.
- You can put a great deal of energy into your children's lives and ambitions – your children will feel valued and recognised.
- You are predictable and supportive – your children can rely on you.

Type 9

- You are a peacemaker – you promote a harmonious environment and this has a calming influence on your family.

> *Sometimes the kids complained that they didn't trust Kerry's opinion because she took everyone's side. The problem was that she could really understand how everyone else saw things and that made it difficult for her to know what her opinion really was.*
>
> *Kerry was very uncomfortable with any conflict in the home. She would tend to agree with whatever the children wanted, rather than have to confront them. When they asked her to do something, she could not say no, even though she knew she didn't want to do it and really had no intention of doing it. It was less effort just to say yes in the moment and hope they would change their minds and forget about it.*

How your type adversely affects your children

The potential negative effects of being a Type Nine parent include:

- Your avoidance of conflict can feel to your children like important issues are minimised and not dealt with.
- You can control others with passive-aggressive behaviours, such as being stubborn and obstinate.
- Your tendency to tune out from what is going on around you can look like you are disengaging from the family.

- You can explode with anger from time to time, which can be frightening and unsettling for you and your family.
- You may be too permissive and not give your children clear directives.
- You can too readily merge with your children's agendas and smother their independence.
- Your procrastination can affect your children's opportunities.

> *Even though Kerry enjoyed family life, there were times when she felt there was too much drain on her energy. She found making decisions difficult and keeping to schedules tiring. With the constant hustle and bustle of family life, she sometimes found it difficult to be her easygoing, relaxed self. She could spend a whole afternoon reading a book, oblivious to what was going on around her. It was like she was asleep on the inside, even though she was awake.*

Type 9

What causes you stress as a parent

Being a parent can be stressful for everyone, but there are particular aspects of parenting that tend to increase the stress of Nines. These include:

- feeling under pressure to make a decision or get something done
- when there is conflict and fighting in the home.
- when your children get impatient with you for not making a decision
- worrying too much about what others are thinking of you
- feeling confused about what you really want, which causes you to procrastinate

Type 9

- wasting hours watching television while putting off the exertion needed to get things done
- your children taking advantage of you
- everyone telling you what to do
- having to say yes when you really want to say no
- not feeling listened to or noticed
- being hard on yourself for lacking discipline or initiative.

Type Nine variations

Arrows

As we described in Step One, the arrows on the Enneagram give an indication of how – under certain circumstances – our behaviour can change from what is usual for our primary type. Under strain we move towards our 'stress point' and when relaxed we draw on the resources from our 'security point'.

9. The Accommodator

Typically, when a Type Nine is under stress they will take on the negative aspects of a Type Six and when feeling safe and secure they will take on the positive aspects of a Type Three. We suggest you read the list at the beginning of the Type Three and Type Six chapters, describing strengths and challenges, to explore more about your stress and security points.

The Accommodator and Peacemaker

Wings

As with all types, the number on either side of your core type can influence and 'flavour' your behaviour. We call these your wings.

Type Nine parents tend to vary in their personalities, depending on their dominant 'wing':

- Nines with a more developed Eight wing tend to be more outgoing, assertive and anti-authoritarian. They have the ability to be both powerful and gentle. On the downside, they may vacillate between being confrontational and conciliatory. They can be stubborn and defensive and dig their heels in, refusing to listen to anyone.
- Nines with a more developed One wing tend to be more orderly, reserved and less prone to speak up until they have things sorted out. They are generally more disciplined than the above wing. On the downside, they can be critical, emotionally controlled and compliant. They are less adventurous and more reserved.

> *"An eye for an eye only ends up making the whole world blind"*
> – Mahatma Gandhi

Type 9

What will enhance your self-mastery

As a Type Nine there are things you can practise that will help break down less resourceful habits and increase your self-mastery. As you stay present to these habits you become more aware and will be able to make bet-ter choices in the ways that you re-spond. Ultimately this will benefit all your relationships.

- Focus more on your own needs and desires and practise being more direct and clear about them.
- Take more control of your own life and live less through your children's lives.
- Develop more self-confi-dence and worry less about what others are thinking about you.
- Understand and accept that some conflict is okay and can often lead to a positive outcome.
- Take steps to become more energetic by incorporating a regular routine of physical exercise to help increase your efficiency and productivity.
- Practise staying present to yourself and being aware of when you are tuning out.

Type 9

The Accommodator and Peacemaker

Parenting strategies for growth

As mentioned in the introduction to this section, this is perhaps the most important part of this chapter. Challenging yourself to practise some of the following tips and strategies will help you grow as a parent. We suggest that you try out a small number of these strategies initially. There is no need to follow them in order: start with the ones that seem easiest. Try to build them into the way you communicate and interact with your children. Choose just one a week if you like, noticing what impact the change has on your relationship and interactions with your family.

1. **Speak your own truth:** Learn to recognise what you really want and to let others know what it is. When you speak up for yourself you will become more decisive and confident and able to set clearer guidelines for yourself and your children. Practise saying, "What I really think is …" and "What I'd most like is …"

2. **It's okay to say no:** Notice when you say yes when you really want to say no. Practise giving yourself permission to be aware of what you need. It is okay to say no instead of trying to please everyone.

3. **Resolve conflict in a positive way:** Learn to accept that it is normal and necessary to have some conflict in the family. Rather than avoiding it or tuning out, practise bringing your mediation skills into the situation.

4. **Wake up!** Become more aware of when you use distractions like television to zone out from doing

Type 9

what you need to do. The longer you procrastinate the more pressure you put on yourself, because tasks accumulate. Things that seemed unimportant then become urgent, which can lead to feelings of paralysis and of being overwhelmed. Practise increasing your awareness of when you might be zoning out – stop the habit and move the task or decision back onto your priority list.

5. **Notice your energy levels:** Take greater responsibility for your energy and notice when you start to feel it draining away. At those times, practise turning up your energy: be decisive and acknowledge the emotion (which may be anger) that can help increase your energy.

6. **Just do it:** Learn to get things done on time, recognising that some stress is okay and can help you think clearly. Choose some tasks that need doing, or decisions that need making, and tell yourself: "Just do it … *now!*"

7. **Create your own boundaries:** Start to recognise when you are merging with your children's lives and living through them. Be clear in your expectations and clarify your boundaries to encourage your children's independence.

Type 9

Parenting together

Many 'experts' talk about the importance of a unified approach to parenting between parents or partners. Conflict arises when parents do not agree about what is necessary to their children's upbringing and what is important in the family dynamics.

It should be clear by now that such conflict is quite understandable. Two parents will usually have different Enneagram types and, therefore, different preferred parenting styles. As we have seen, what is very important to a parent of one type may have very little importance to a parent of a different type. As friction arises, it becomes difficult for both parents to know whether to back down or stand their ground.

For example, a Type One mother may insist on tidiness and order in the home as well as expecting her children to behave 'properly', especially in company. This could be stressful for the family, the mother's anxiety rising as she tries to get the children to do what she asks and behave the way she expects. It could be exacerbated if the father in this family were a Type Nine. He would probably not see these issues as worth stressing over, as his greatest desire would be to have a conflict-free environment. He may tune out completely, not support his wife or even undermine what she is trying to achieve by telling her to chill out and leave the kids alone. Clearly this situation would send mixed messages from the parents to the children, and it certainly would not exemplify a unified approach! And this is just one example of the many possible challenges between parents of different Enneagram types.

While it is difficult (but understandable) that we don't

always see eye to eye with our partner, understanding each other's personalities can be very insightful. The Enneagram is useful here in demonstrating what motivates the thoughts, feelings and behaviours that each parent brings to their parenting.

Having a deeper awareness of your own personality and a willingness to understand the personality of your partner can help in creating a parenting approach that is more unified. Developing your emotional intelligence, as we outlined earlier, involves finding ways of working together with others and having the ability to recognise, understand and manage emotions in yourself.

Choosing to learn about your partner's personality style and what is important to them can help alleviate some of the problems associated with differing points of view. You may understand why something is very important to your partner and so choose to show empathy and support their approach. Next time, they may recognise something that is very important to you and be willing to support you in the same way. One useful feature when you apply the Enneagram in parenting together is understanding that you should not consider your partner 'wrong' just because they see things differently from you.

Of course, this depends on a degree of compromise. If one parent constantly insists that their way is the right way and is never willing to see the other's point of view, it will cause resentment and conflict between the parents, which will flow through to the children. The risk is that one parent opts out of the parenting process altogether. We encourage both parents to discover their Enneagram type, and to read each other's relevant chapter above. This will bring both of you new insights

165

into each other's motivations and why each of you does what you do.

Single parenting

Single parenting can create unique challenges, particularly if an ex-partner insists on undermining your parenting style. There may also be another partner, step-parents, grandparents or carers involved in your child's parenting. A key point here is that we cannot control another person's behaviour and cannot change them. By concentrating on making your own 'above-the-line' parenting choices, you may be able to educate or influence the other parent without confrontation. We are responsible only for our own behaviour.

Explore

FIRST DATE

Step Three

Unlock your child's potential

The nine keys to unlocking your child's potential

Every child is born with their own unique temperament – an aspect of their personality that was genetically coded from conception. As they interact with their environment and their nurturing and protective figures – particularly their parents, in most cases – a child's whole personality develops. Eventually, somewhere between the ages of 10 and 15, the

169

child's dominant Enneagram type is set and does not change. However, this does not mean that their responses to the world and their behaviours are 'locked in'. These will vary through life, depending on a combination of their level of stress and their level of self-mastery (i.e. their ability to respond to that stress). As we described in Step One, when a person (a child, teenager or adult) is subjected to stress but does not have the self-awareness or self-mastery to identify and deal with that stress, they will often display undesirable behaviours that disconnect them from a sense of wellbeing.

To support and guide our children into flourishing young adults we need to address the complex system that is the human being and help them build self-awareness and self-mastery. This could, of course, be the subject of another complete book. But rather than make this too complex, we will introduce you to the nine keys that will unlock your child's potential. While each of the keys is associated with one of the nine Enneagram types, they can be broadly applied. They are universal principles that, when present and operating, greatly contribute to a child's ability to survive and thrive in their world. Each of the nine keys is necessary in the development of the 'whole' child. Developing and nurturing all the nine keys will assist your children in flourishing, that is, achieving the highest level of happiness and wellbeing.

Parenting is a multifaceted job. It is probably one of the most challenging yet most rewarding jobs you will ever have. We believe these are the nine fundamental areas you can work on as a parent that will support your child's growth, development, happiness and wellbeing.

How to use the nine keys

Over the years, as we have developed our parent-coaching businesses, we have designed and refined the nine keys to be a simple yet effective action plan for parents. As you read through the keys you will discover there are practices to enhance each key within your children. Within each key there are activities created for you, the parent, to practise and put into action over a period of time. We suggest that you start at the first key and slowly make your way through all nine in order. Take time to pause every couple of weeks or so, noting how you are doing and how your children are responding.

In most instances this is about you, the parent, trying on a new way of being to support the flourishing of your children. It is about what you are doing 'with' yourself and your children – not what you are doing 'to' your children.

You can start to experiment with the nine keys immediately. Even if you are still working out your Enneagram parenting personality, these keys will provide you with new ways to build connected relationships with your children.

How you practise these will depend greatly on the age of your children, your family's lifestyle and, of course, your personality. Take a fluid approach, practise with each key and observe what happens. Enjoy creating some new habits within your family.

Key 1: Develop mutual respect

The word respect can be defined as "to treat with special consideration or high regard" (see Sterling 2008, p.51). Notice that the word *deserve* does not appear in the definition. Everyone is born worthy of respect; it is something that all people need and want. Acknowledging respect for someone is an affirmation of their being. We can communicate respect to our children in many different ways. Respect comes across in our words, our body language and our attentiveness (see Key 2 below). Unfortunately in today's society many adults believe they must be respected simply because they are adults. The key here is that respect is mutual. If you show respect for another then they will show respect for you.

Practices to enhance this key:

a. Strengths spotting: Create a list of the strengths or qualities you respect or admire in your children. Putting accomplishments aside, what particular strengths do you respect them for? When you are with your children, start using words that describe these strengths or qualities, with less focus on the actual achievement and more on the strength or quality.

b. Shift your attention to something that your children have done well and think about the strength or quality they used. Then consciously set out to tell them, at least once a day over the next few weeks, how you respect, admire or value that strength in them. At the end of each day, sit quietly and ask yourself how you used the word 'respect' in relation to their strength today and what was the result, for both you and your children.

c. Encourage discussion in your family around principles, fairness and justice, and a respect for order.

Key 2: Nurture deep listening

The definition of listening is, "to make a conscious effort to hear; to attend to closely, so as to hear". We can show our children that we are hearing what they are saying by actively listening to them and not just passively responding. The attention needs to be on the child and what they are saying, rather than on us trying to give them advice. They are actually working things out for themselves by talking them out. As they feel heard and understood, mutual respect is developed and they will feel loved, appreciated and safe in sharing what is important to them. This also helps them feel connected to you and develops a warm and trusting relationship. In turn, your children will learn to listen more deeply and attentively to others and show care to them – an important life skill.

Practices to enhance this key:

a. Listen to your children when they open up, without trying to solve their problems. Allow them to talk without interrupting them and practise listening to what they are saying without criticism or judgement. "Listen with your lips shut."

b. Whenever possible, stop whatever you are doing when

Unlock

your children want to talk to you. Offer them your full, undivided attention and practise listening to really understand what they are saying from their point of view.

c. Set some time aside from your busy schedule so you can be available to spend some time with your children without distraction. You may need to turn off your mobile phone and other devices! Offer to help with homework or just have a conversation. Again, concentrate on listening to understand, rather than to fix or solve a problem. It is often in their speaking out that a child is able to process whatever is on their mind.

Key 3: Realise their full potential

Many school mottos have messages around striving for personal best. For a child to discover their talents and reach their potential, they first need to feel good about themselves and have high self-esteem. Encouraging your children to improve their skills is a healthy, natural component of parenting. However, it can be overdone, with encouragement becoming, in the child's eyes, nagging, pushing and driving too hard. Always be aware of whether or not you are striking the right balance.

Practices to enhance this key:

a. Talk to your children about goals. Help them to imagine new possibilities. Get them to visualise the way things might be and how they would feel if they reached a goal. Support them in the way that *they* need. Avoid mapping out your children's life for them – that creates dependency or resentment and it doesn't take into account their unique hopes and dreams for life. Open up regular conversations about the future and how they imagine it.

b. Work on making your children feel good about themselves. Start to shift your pride away from yourself and onto your child. Replace "I'm so proud of you for getting an A" with "I respect the hard work you put in to get that grade". Use the strengths you identified in Key 1 above. Find a way to acknowledge all the contributions your children make to your family in this way.

c. Encourage your children to explore and get creative about their talents. Acknowledge their interests, especially when they are different from yours. Be open and flexible as they try new things. Provide them with opportunities to demonstrate what they can do by using their strengths.

Key 4: Develop identity and appreciation

Children, just like adults, have a human need to understand themselves and their feelings. Your children need to be appreciated for who they are. This will allow them to really get to know themselves as individuals. When they feel appreciated they will know you support them, and they'll be learning how to appreciate others and the world around them.

One of the fundamental building blocks of a parent–child relationship is love. Parents nearly always love their children, but this love may not be expressed in a way that the children can feel. Showing appreciation helps parents focus effectively on meeting a child's emotional need for love and 'filling up their love tank' (which gets depleted regularly). One of the best ways to show appreciation is by determining your children's 'love language'. There are five basic love languages of children, and below is a brief introduction to them as identified by author and relationship expert Dr Gary Chapman. Discover your child's primary love language and you will find the most effective way to keep their emotional love tank full.

The five love languages

It's easy to tell when a child wants to be loved. Getting the message across is another matter entirely. In addition to the obvious generation gap, many parents and children face a language barrier when it comes to emotions like love. The *Five Love Languages of Children* by Dr Gary Chapman and Dr Ross Campbell and *The Five Love Languages of Teenagers* by Dr Gary Chapman (2010) are invaluable tools for analysing a child's love language and expressing your affections in an effective way. For a child to feel the love of their parents is an incredible gift, but not always one that is well received if given in the wrong 'language'. However, if you can speak the right language the difference can seem miraculous. The five love languages of children are, briefly, as follows.

Quality time

Quality time is giving your undivided attention to your child;

for example, taking a walk with them, playing a board game, or watching a sporting event.

Gifts

Don't mistake this love language for materialism. The receiver of gifts thrives on the love, thoughtfulness and effort behind the gift – not its monetary value. A gift is any visible, tangible symbol of love. It need not be expensive.

Words of affirmation

Some children literally need to hear things like "I really appreciate your help" and "Thanks for unpacking the dishwasher". If this is your child's primary love language, be careful not to patronise.

Physical touch

A genuine hug or rubbing their shoulders will keep them happy for the rest of the day. Loving expressions of physical touch could include fixing your daughter's hair or playfully sparring with your son.

Acts of service

These are things that you don't normally do for your children. For example, if your child always catches the bus home you might pick them up occasionally. It also includes teaching and learning activities like showing your child how to check the pressure on the tyres or leading them through the steps of making a meal.

Unlock

The fact of parenting is that most parents do not naturally speak their child's primary love language. If it's not clear to you which love language is primary to your child, it may be because they have a close secondary love language as well. Most people do. This approach can be applied to other areas of your life, as well. Consider your relationships with your spouse, colleagues and peers. In any of these situations you'll be pleasantly surprised at what happens when you appreciate others in their primary love language.

Practices to enhance this key:

a. Encourage your children to talk about their feelings. Model this to them by telling them how you feel about things. Be authentic in this – if you feel frustrated or sad, then say that. Encourage your family to express their emotions, and truly listen and reflect back when they do.

b. Be careful not to take your children's efforts and contributions for granted. Incorporate the word 'appreciate' into your vocabulary: "I appreciate the way you …" Learn to value your children for *their* unique contribution to the world. That might mean suspending your own judgement about them.

c. The next time you catch yourself telling a friend or family member how great your children are, make a mental note to tell your children the same.

d. Go here to take the test with your children: www.5lovelanguages.com/profile/

178

Key 5: Develop an understanding of self and the world

Our children need to understand how the world works, its laws and principles, and how they can find their place in it. The world is becoming an increasingly more self-indulgent and violent place and children will have many influences in their lives. By raising your children's emotional intelligence, you will support them in becoming decent human beings of good character.

Practices to enhance this key:

a) During a family meeting or meal time, discuss your family's values and how they might differ from those of other families. Encourage discussion around the different interpretations and the importance of respecting differences.

b) Cultivate learning. Encourage a sense of curiosity and expanding knowledge in areas outside your family. Visit other parts of your city, town or country and explore with an open mind as you observe others' differences.

c) Help your children to identify the feelings of others and develop a sensitivity to building empathy. You could use the following approach:

   • *Fact:* state the fact (no judgements) of what they said or did.

   • *Impact:* explain the impact on you and the relationship.

- *Request:* ask how they might be willing to do it differently next time. For example: "When you raise your voice and walk away, I feel disrespected and hurt. It makes me less likely to help you next time. Would you be willing to speak to me next time in a way that is more caring and respectful?"

Key 6: Develop a sense of belonging and responsibility

To be responsible is to be trustworthy. We need to prepare our children to eventually manage life on their own by encouraging them to accept an increasing amount of responsibility. If you want your children to do specific chores in the home, get alongside them and show them what to do. Take time to talk with them about your expectation and remove any ambiguity (for example, what does "tidy your room" really mean to you?). When setting a new responsibility, don't assume they know how to do even a simple task without instruction. Remember to use Key 2 as well: stop and listen to their suggestions. There may be more than one 'right' way of doing the chore. By giving your children responsibilities, they see how they are valued. This gives them a sense of worth and a sense of belonging to the family. Your children need to understand that they are part of a greater whole and that they can give support to and receive support from the family, other groups and society.

Practices to enhance this key:

a. Agreements can be a great way to encourage your children to become responsible. Use language that does

180

not sound like you are giving orders, such as, "I'd like to make an agreement" or "I have a request". Make a clear request and ask them if they can agree to it. You may need to negotiate until an agreement is reached. However, know your bottom line and once a request is agreed upon, expect your children to be responsible and get it done.

b. Demonstrate a specific task with your children, such as teaching them to use the washing machine. You might consider writing a step-by-step guide and sticking it next to the machine so they feel confident to do the task by themselves when you are not around. Set them up for success.

c. Have a 'how the house runs' brainstorming session with the family. Sit everyone down and, on a big piece of paper, brainstorm everything you can think of that has to be done to keep the house 'running', for example, shopping, putting groceries away, preparing food, setting the table, sorting washing, washing, folding, ironing, emptying rubbish to the outside bins, putting the bins out, bringing mail in, walking and feeding the dog, etc. Once the list is complete, tick off who currently does what – usually Mum does a lot! Ask which chores each person would like to be responsible for on a weekly or monthly basis, with the aim of evening out the responsibility. Make an agreement around the new responsibilities.

Unlock

Key 7: Develop independence and resilience

Resilience is the ability to bounce back and keep going in the face of adversity. To be resilient and independent we need to learn how to adapt to change. The sooner we allow our children to experience and cope with change, disappointment, mistakes and learning, the sooner they'll develop their own resilience strategies. In essence this means letting go of some of your control and encouraging your children to make their own choices. This can be easier to do for some personalities than others!

Practices to enhance this key:

a. Start with yourself and take a look in the mirror. How do you model resilience to your children? Work out how you navigate change and lead from there so your children can learn from you. Turn up the volume on your skills of being optimistic, positive and realistic.

b. Encourage independence. Be on the lookout for opportunities for your children to take on more responsibility and act independently.

c. Say the words "What do you choose?" or "What will your choice be?" when your children present you with a problem. Choices can be made about what they think, say and do. There's often no right or wrong answer, so give up thinking that it's you who needs to provide all the answers. Let your children brain-storm their own choices – open them up to their own solutions.

Key 8: Build empowerment and confidence

Building a sense of authority and empowerment is key to developing confidence and raising the emotional health of your children. Today's parents want their children to gain a sense of inner confidence, courage and strength to successfully surmount whatever life presents. This means we need to guide them to persevere when obstacles arise in childhood – as they always do – such as bullies, failed grades, mistakes, disappointments and bruises. Such inner strength will also support them as they pursue their dreams. Building empowerment is important in the development of a child's self-confidence, self-worth and self-esteem. How you respond and teach them to bounce back from setbacks and challenges will greatly influence their own abilities. Children observe your language and your behaviour as you come across tricky situations and failures; their life lessons start very early. You have great opportunities to influence their thinking and model a positive mindset.

Practices to enhance this key:

a. Allow your children to make decisions and experience the consequences. Providing choice is the first step to developing a sense of autonomy.

b. Develop confidence by encouraging your children to take part in activities that shift them out of their comfort zone while allowing them to achieve and be successful.

c. Appreciate your children's unique point of view and encourage them to express their ideas and beliefs without judging or criticising.

183

Unlock

Key 9: Encourage stability and groundedness

All people need to find peace of mind, stability and groundedness in an ever-changing world. Supporting your children physically, mentally, emotionally and spiritually will help them find these qualities in themselves. Show that you care for them by supporting interests that add to their life experience and nurture their potential.

For young people to become stable and grounded requires their parents to let go and allow them to find their own feet. We've become a generation of helicopter parents with a tendency to rescue rather than support. When your children make a mistake, or are going through a difficult time, resist the temptation to rescue them. Instead, ask them what kind of support they need (not necessarily from you) and then allow them to work it out for themselves. The type and level of support you offer should change as your children mature.

Practices to enhance this key:

a. Write a list of the ways you support your children financially, emotionally, physically, spiritually and intellectually. Note any areas that need more support and, with your children in mind, create ways that you can provide it.

b. Spending a good quantity of time with your children encourages good conversation. Create a tradition in the form of a regular outing with each one of your children without other adults or distractions. A minimum of two to four hours is needed, say once a quarter, spent on a fun activity with focused reflection – and without electronics.

c. Show your children that you are there for them by including the word 'support' in your conversation. Ask directly: "What kind of support do you need to complete/assist/do/get over ..." Refrain from being critical or defensive when your children say what they need. Pay attention to listening to them well.

Conclusion

The journey of parenthood is filled with challenges and great opportunities, not only for the child, but for the parent as well. Understanding your Enneagram type is a great way to enhance that journey to deeper awareness and closer relationships. A cautionary note, however: as we discussed back in Step One, you must refrain from stereotyping or labelling your children. When people initially discover the Enneagram there is a tendency to try to type those around them. This may lead to incorrect typing and assumptions based on outwardly displayed behaviours, rather than on the internal motivations that drive those behaviours.

The important work you do as a result of reading this book is to *discover* and *explore* your own Enneagram type and better understand yourself as a parent. We wish you many 'aha', light bulb moments.. While you do this, understand that there are people of the eight other types who you will be interacting with – including your partner if you have one – and that your type will interact with and affect each of them differently. We are ultimately only responsible for our own behaviour and we can learn to maximise our positives and minimise the negatives to have even better relationships with our families.

Enjoy getting to know yourself and them!

References and recommended reading

Baron, R & Wagele, E 1994, *The Enneagram Made Easy*. HarperCollins, NY.

Chapman, G 2010, *The Five Love Languages of Teenagers*. Northfield Publishing, IL.

Chapman, G & Campbell, R 1997, *The Five Love Languages of Children*. Northfield Publishing, IL.

Daniels, D & Price, V 2009, *The Essential Enneagram: The definitive personality test and self-discovery guide*. Revised and updated. HarperCollins, NY.

Howe-Murphy, R 2007, *Deep Coaching: Using the Enneagram as a catalyst for profound change*. Enneagram Press, CA.

Lapid-Bogda, G 2004, *Bringing Out the Best in Yourself at Work: How to use the Enneagram system for success*. McGraw Hill, NY.

Lapid-Bogda, G 2009, *Bringing Out the Best in Everyone You Coach: Use the Enneagram system for exceptional results*. McGraw Hill, NY.

Palmer, H 1991, *The Enneagram: Understanding yourself and the others in your life*. HarperCollins, NY

Rohr, R Ebert, A 1992 *Discovering the Enneagram: An ancient tool for a spiritual journey*. Crossroads, NY

Riso, D & Hudson, R 1999, *The Wisdom of the Enneagram: The complete guide to psychological and spiritual growth for the nine personality types*. Bantam Books, NY.

Riso, D & Hudson, R 2000, *Understanding the Enneagram: The practical guide to personality types*. Houghton Mifflin Company, NY.

Sterling, D 2008, *The Parent as Coach Approach*. White Oak Publishing, NM.

Wagele, E 1997, *The Enneagram of Parenting: The 9 types of children and how to raise them successfully*. Harper, CA.

Wagele, E 2007, *Finding the Birthday Cake: Helping children raise their self-esteem*. New Horizon Press, NJ.

Wagner, JP 2010, *Nine Lenses on the World: The Enneagram perspective*. Nine Lens Press, IL.

About the authors

Tracy Tresidder

Tracy's personal vision is 'to change the world one family at a time'. She is passionate about assisting people to lead a conscious life through deeper understanding of the Enneagram.

Tracy has dedicated the past 13 years working as a university educator, coach, speaker and author to assisting and supporting individuals and families through the turbulent times that life presents so they are able to experience more loving and healthy relationships.

She has been studying the Enneagram with some of the world's best teachers in the area over the last 11 years. This has helped Tracy to move to a deeper level of exploration and understanding – not only of herself as a coach but also of her coaching clients, particularly parents and their teenagers.

Tracy coaches parents and teenagers to develop greater awareness by understanding their Enneagram style. This helps them improve their communication and connection, and develop relationships that are mutually respectful, loving and trusting. She also facilitates communication and leadership workshops with corporations to raise consciousness and increase leadership capability. This empowers participants to make intentional choices, to connect with others differently and to achieve their desired outcomes.

Tracy lives in Sydney, Australia with her wonderful family: husband Mike and sons Adam and Ben.

Her qualifications and awards include: BEd, MEd, Professional Certified Coach (PCC), International Coach Federation 2009 Coach of the Year (NSW), Immediate Past President ICF Australasia, ICF assessor and member, University of Sydney Coaching and Mentoring Association member, Certified Enneagram Teacher (ESNT), International Enneagram Association Accredited Teacher and professional member.

Margaret Loftus

Margaret is an experienced teacher, counsellor, spiritual director, certified coach, workshop facilitator, author and speaker. Her expertise includes working with parents and teenagers to strengthen relationships, and coaching those in the workplace around issues of self-awareness, self-management and emotional maturity.

Margaret brings the wisdom of the Enneagram to develop greater individual insight and deeper levels of awareness and personal understanding. She has trained with internationally-recognised teachers over many years. Her objective is to move people toward discovering their authentic self, which is often hidden beneath the constructs of their performing self. This can bring to life the gifts of one's essential nature and encourage personal transformation.

In educational settings, Margaret uses the Enneagram to promote emotional intelligence, which is essential when working with teachers, parents, teenagers and young adults. As a qualified and experienced teacher herself, Margaret recognises the stresses and problems parents face in their genuine desire to be good at the parenting role. She is very enthusiastic about helping parents to develop a deeper awareness of themselves, which can mean more authentic and connected relationships with their children.

Margaret's skills and insights are also applicable in businesses and organisations where there is a desire for change and transformation. As individuals develop a greater understanding of themselves and others, relationships improve and the working environment is enhanced.

Margaret lives in Melbourne, is married to Peter and has three wonderful children: Rachel, Georgie and Jonathan.

Margaret's qualifications include: BEd; Grad Dip Couns; Spiritual Direction; Cert IV Life Coaching (ICF accredited); NLP Practitioner; Professional Member of the International Enneagram Association; and Certified Enneagram Teacher (ESNT).

Jacqui Pollock

Jacqui has a relentless passion for helping people to discover the very best within themselves so they can bring out the best in others. This is the purpose of her work, which she brings alive within the board-rooms, schools and living rooms of Australia.

Jacqui is an inspirational workshop facilitator, leadership and family coach, author and speaker. She helps leaders and parents to expand their emotional intelligence so they stay resourceful in their challenging relationship moments.

Within the education sector, Jacqui facilitates workshops and coaches school principals and Department of Education executives. She helps people find the best in themselves so they can lead and inspire their teams and students. Jacqui coaches diverse groups within global and local businesses, from undergraduates to senior leaders, across Australia and Asia.

Jacqui works extensively with parents and families, supporting them to build connected and authentic relationships. She runs workshops and personalised programs for parents and teens. Jacqui brings the wisdom of the Enneagram into families; she believes that learning about your Enneagram type as a parent can help put your relationships into perspective and provide new choices, rather than relying on worn out ways of coping.

Jacqui lives in Sydney with her husband, Jack, and their amazing teenagers, Zoe and Fred.

Jacqui is a Business Studies graduate, professionally trained coach through Coach U (ICF accredited) and a certified practitioner of Neuro Linguistic Programming (NLP). She is an International Coach Federation member and Professional Member of the International Enneagram Association.

Made in the USA
San Bernardino, CA
31 July 2017